12.95

12.95

# THE ALLIED FORCES IN ITALY
## 1943-45

# THE ALLIED FORCES IN ITALY
## 1943-45

### GUIDO ROSIGNOLI

A DAVID & CHARLES MILITARY BOOK

**British Library Cataloguing in Publication Data**

Rosignoli, Guido
    The Allied forces in Italy 1943–45. – (A
David & Charles military book)
    1. World War 2. Italian campaign. Army
operations by Allied forces
    I. Title
    940.54′21

    ISBN 0-7153-9212-3

Book designed by Michael Head

First published 1989

Typeset by Typesetters (Birmingham) Ltd,
Smethwick, West Midlands
**Printed in Portugal**

for David & Charles Publishers plc
Brunel House   Newton Abbot   Devon

Distributed in the United States by
Sterling Publishing Co. Inc,
2, Park Avenue, New York, NY10016

# Contents

ITALIAN CAMPAIGN
ENDS MAY 2, 1945

5TH REACHES SWITZERLAND
at COMO APRIL 29, 1945

Brenner
Pass

MILAN ENTERED
APRIL 29, 1945

VENICE APRIL 29, 1945

FERRARA FALLS APRIL 23 1945

5TH CROSSES PO APRIL 23 1945

BOLOGNA SEIZED
APRIL 21, 1945

RAVENNA DEC. 5, 1944

LAST GREAT OFFENSIVE
STARTS APRIL 14, 1945

8TH IN RIMINI SEPT 22, 1944

LA SPEZIA TAKEN APRIL 23, 1945
GENOA APRIL 27, 1945

8TH CLEARS FLORENCE
AUG. 12, 1944

ANCONA JULY 18, 1944

PISA CAPTURED SEPT. 2, 1944

FUTA PASS CLEARED SEPT 24, 1944

LEGHORN SEIZED JULY 19 1944

ITALY

ROME ENTERED
JUNE 4, 1944

BATTLE FOR CASSINO BEGINS
FEB. 21, 1944 - CASSINO
CAPTURED MAY 18, 1944

8TH TAKES AIRFIELDS
AT FOGGIA SEPT. 27, 1943

BEACHHEAD BREAKS OUT
AT CISTERNA MAY 25, 1944

ANZIO BEACHHEAD ESTABLISHED
JAN. 22, 1944 - JUNCTION WITH
MAIN 5TH ARMY FORCES MAY 25

BIG PUSH AT MINTURNO
STARTS MAY 11, 1944

JUNCTION AT VALLO
SEPT. 17, 1943

VOLTURNO CROSSED AT
CAPUA OCT. 1, 1943

SARDINIA OCCUPIED SEPT. 18, 1943
CORSICA OCT. 5, 1943

NAPLES TAKEN OCT. 1, 1943

5TH ARMY LANDS IN
SALERNO BAY SEPT. 9, 1943

MEDITERRANEAN

PALERMO FALLS
JULY 22, 1943

SICILIAN CAMPAIGN ENDS
AT MESSINA AUG. 17, 1943

TARANTO LANDING
SEPT. 9, 1943

8TH STARTS INVASION
OF ITALY SEPT. 3, 1943

SICILY

ALGERIA

SICILIAN CAMPAIGN
BEGINS JULY 9, 1943

TUNISIAN CAMPAIGN
ENDS MAY 13, 1943

SEA

MALTA

TUNISIA

MILES
0 20 40 60 80 100

# List of Maps

# Foreword

Field Marshal the Viscount Montgomery of Alamein, KG, dedicated forty-one of the 550 pages of his war memoirs to describing the operations in Sicily and Italy, up to the Sangro river. Italy was a secondary front compared with North-Western Europe where the Allies deployed over twenty armoured divisions. In Italy there were only four, later three.

The Allied Forces in Italy were the most cosmopolitan organisation ever to fight on a battlefield. Although the main contingents were British and American, the Allied Forces included Canadians, New Zealanders, South Africans, Indians, Poles, French, Algerians, Moroccans and troops from other French colonial territories, Brazilians, Greeks, Palestinians, Jewish and, of course, Italians. The Royal Air Force included Australian and Yugoslav squadrons and volunteers from all over the world.

I was ten years old at that time and the first clear memories of my life relate to this age of turmoil and destruction that was the end of World War Two. Bomb holes remained unfilled and roofs uncovered as any effort to repair damage, to restore life to normality had become futile. It seemed that the war would go on and on for ever until everything was destroyed in an uncontrollable, senseless frenzy that no one could stop. By the end of April 1945 almost everything had been destroyed, bombed or blown up; there was no electric power, no running water; people lived barricaded in their homes waiting for the next invader.

A single armoured car of the 12th Lancers, the 2nd New Zealand Division's recce regiment, arrived in my town – I admired the courage of these men who entered a foreign, enemy town, miles ahead of their own forces. There were no flags, no applause. The vehicle halted in a square. The soldiers sat on top of it talking and smoking while a radio was buzzing inside. A silent group of civilians assembled around them and my father asked for a cigarette, but he did not smoke it, as a real cigarette was a precious gift in those days. I was gazing at the soldiers in amazement . . . where did they come from? Previously I had seen Germans, Russian Cossacks and Mongols, Yugoslav Chetniks with long hair. The German propaganda had told us that the Allied soldiers were bloodthirsty Negroes and Moroccans, but these men looked like us. As television did not yet exist we had no idea of what our 'enemies' looked like! After a few minutes the soldiers re-entered the armoured car, which turned around on its way back.

God only knows what would have happened if Field Marshal Alexander, a few weeks later, had not ordered the forced occupation of the town, which was personally led by General Clark.

Some marvellous months followed. I still remember the tanks, some enormous lorries with a dozen wheels and the jeeps, hundreds of jeeps! There were Scots wearing kilts, Indians with different turbans, white and black Americans, all with colourful badges. Thousands were there and I thought that it was extremely lucky for me that they had decided to congregate there, from Britain, New Zealand, India and America. These soldiers did not harass, deport and kill people, as all our previous invaders had done.

Later, I learned that chance had brought them and all they wanted was to go back home. They did not look as martial as the Germans, nor did they boast about battles and victories, although they were the victors. Many of them had been at Salerno, Cassino, Anzio and on the 'Gothic' Line, but they were still men, before being soldiers.

I would like this to be a book for the soldiers who were there. Their units are listed and the formations of which these units were part, their badges are shown with pictures of their leaders and comrades. In these pages they can follow again that dangerous march up the Italian peninsula and perhaps this book will help them to recollect some memories.

That is all I wish to achieve.

G. ROSIGNOLI

# I The Invasion of Sicily

The decision to invade Sicily was made at the Casablanca Conference in January 1943, well before hostilities in North Africa ceased on 9 May, 1943. The invasion was code named Operation HUSKY.

The Combined Chiefs of Staff of the Allied forces nominated General Dwight D. Eisenhower as Supreme Commander and General Sir Harold Alexander as Deputy Supreme Commander. Admiral of the Fleet Sir Andrew Cunningham became the naval commander and Air Chief Marshal Sir Arthur Tedder the air commander.

On 11 February, Eisenhower appointed General Bernard L. Montgomery to command the Eastern Task Force, known as Force 545 – the British 8th Army – and Lt-General George S. Patton to lead the Western Task Force, Force 343, which consisted at that time of the 2nd US Corps, later upgraded to 7th US Army. Both Forces were supervised by Force 141, which became 15th Army Group, commanded by Lord Alexander.

The central planning for HUSKY started immediately at Algiers and within the British and American task forces in Cairo and Rabat, respectively. Plans for the invasion of Sicily and Sardinia had been considered earlier as the two islands were the obvious stepping stones to Southern Europe. Nevertheless, the Allies faced many problems. The landing forces selected for this operation could not all be assembled in Tunisia. They would have to come from the Middle East, North Africa and Britain, but at least the first waves of troops had to land according to a predetermined, precise schedule.

As intelligence on the island's defences was rather defective, the initial landing plans were based on the priority of capturing as many harbours and airfields as possible, but this would have dispersed the Allied forces dangerously. Montgomery envisaged landing his army on the south-eastern coast, with the Americans on its left flank, and capturing the south-east corner of the island, with the ports of Syracuse, Augusta and Catania as supply intakes for his army. On 13 May, scarcely two months before its execution, his plan was accepted by the Combined Chiefs of Staff.

Members of the 209th Company, RASC, wearing khaki drill with shorts, an order of dress used in Italy in summer. As all are wearing the field service cap, this indicates that the photograph was taken before the end of September 1943. *H. B. Stokes Collection*

## THE OPPOSING FORCES IN SICILY

### The Axis Forces
The Axis forces in Sicily were grouped into the 6th Italian Army formed by six divisions, plus some Italian coastal formations of

negligible value. The 12th Corps, deployed on the western side of the island, comprised two Italian divisions and one German. The 16th Corps defended the east of Sicily with one Italian and two German divisions.

The army reserve consisted of the Italian 4th Infantry Division 'Livorno', two German tactical groups detached from 15th Division and eleven mobile anti-parachutists groups. The three German divisions were not first class formations, while the Italian divisions had never been in action and, with exception of the 'Livorno' division, had no motor transport.

**The Axis Forces on Sicily**

| The 12th Corps | 16th Corps |
| --- | --- |
| 28th Infantry Division 'Aosta' | 54th Infantry Division 'Napoli' |
| 26th Infantry Division 'Assietta' | Panzer Division 'Hermann Göring' |
| 15th Panzer-Grenadier Division | 'Kampfgruppe Schmaltz' |

## The Allied Forces

Two Allied armies were to land in Sicily, the British 8th and the US 7th commanded by General Bernard Montgomery and Lt-General George Patton respectively. The 8th Army was designated as the Eastern Task Force with British naval and air support; the

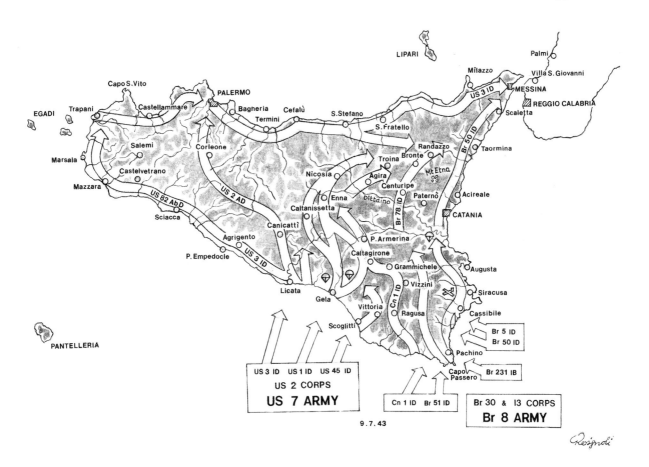

7th Army was designated as the Western Task Force with US naval and air support.

The 8th Army comprised 13th Corps and 30th Corps, each with two divisions, and a reserve of special forces. The 231st Infantry Brigade, the 4th and the 23rd Armoured Brigade were placed under command of one or the other corps or divisions according to necessity. During the campaign, the 78th Infantry Division became part of 30th Corps.

The 7th Army comprised 2nd Corps, with two divisions, an Army Corps, with one division, and a floating reserve and general reserve with three divisions, Rangers and a Moroccan Tabor. A Provisional corps was formed in Sicily and thereafter the divisions were placed under the command of one or the other corps according to necessity. The 4th Moroccan Tabor was attached to the US 3rd, then 1st and subsequently 9th Division during its permanence in Sicily, from 14 July to 18 August 1943.

Bill Gunning, 65th Chemical Warfare Company RE. One platoon of this unit was attached to each of the three British divisions which landed in Sicily while Company HQ landed with the 231st Infantry Brigade. Their task was to provide smoke screens to cover the landing of troops. He wears the 8th Army badge on shoulder-strap slip-ons. *R. Goode Collection*

**The Allied Forces Landing in Sicily**

| **British 8th Army** | **US 7th Army** |
|---|---|
| 13th Corps | 2nd Corps |
|   5th Infantry Division |   1st Infantry Division |
|   50th (Northumbrian) Infantry |   45th Infantry Division 'Thunderbird' |
|     Division | Army Troops |
| 30th Corps |   3rd Infantry Division 'Marne' |
|   1st Canadian Infantry Division | Floating Reserve |
|   51st (Highland) Infantry Division |   2nd Armored Division 'Hell on |
| Reserve |     Wheels' |
|   1st Airborne Division | Reserve |
|   78th Infantry Division |   9th Infantry Division |
|   2nd Special Air Service |   82nd Airborne Division 'All |
|   Special Service Brigade |     American' |
|     (Commandos) |   Rangers |
| |   4th Moroccan Tabor |

## British 8th Army – Field Army

### 1st Canadian Infantry Division

The first units of the 1st Canadian Division arrived in Scotland on 17 December 1939. The division did not join the British Expeditionary Force because it was intended to be sent to Norway but orders were changed and one brigade only was briefly deployed to France before the British evacuation. Some divisional units participated in the Spitzbergen expedition in 1941 and others took part in the Dieppe raid the following year. In June 1943 the division embarked for Sicily.

**1st Canadian Infantry Division**

| 1st Infantry Brigade | Infantry |
|---|---|
|   The Royal Canadian Regiment |   The Seaforth Highlanders of Canada |
|   The Hastings and Prince Edward's |   The Loyal Edmonton Regiment |
|     Regiment | 3rd Infantry Brigade |
|   48th Highlanders of Canada |   Royal 22e Régiment |
| 2nd Infantry Brigade |   The Carleton and York Regiment |
|   Princess Patricia's Canadian Light |   The West Nova Scotia Regiment |

Divisional Troops
Royal Canadian Artillery
   1st (Royal Canadian Horse Artillery),
     2nd and 3rd Field Regiments
   1st Anti-tank Regiment
   2nd Light Anti-aircraft Regiment
Royal Canadian Engineers
   1st, 3rd and 4th Field Company
   2nd Field Park Company

Royal Canadian Signals
   1st Infantry
Reconnaissance Corps
   1st Armoured Car Regiment (The
     Royal Canadian Dragoons)
Machine-gun Battalion
   The Saskatoon Light Infantry

Three examples of AM lire which were legal tender in Italy during the period of the allied invasion. These banknotes were not intended to replace the Italian currency, but to supplement the existing currency in circulation, and were issued by the Allied Forces and the AMG. One hundred thousand million AM lire were issued by 31 December 1945. *G. Rosignoli Collection*

*1st Canadian Army Tank Brigade*
This brigade also went to Sicily, but only the Three Rivers Regiment fought in support of the 1st Canadian Infantry Division. The other two regiments landed at Syracuse at a later stage.

In Sicily, in August 1943, this formation was redesignated 1st Canadian Armoured Brigade and consequently its three army tank regiments were redesignated armoured regiments, as follows:

**1st Canadian Army Tank Brigade**
11th Armoured Regiment (The Ontario
   Regiment)
12th Armoured Regiment (Three
   Rivers Regiment)
14th Armoured Regiment (The Calgary
   Regiment)

'B' Squadron of the 25th Armoured Delivery Regiment, known then as Canadian Tank Delivery Squadron, also landed in Sicily on 17 July 1943.

*5th Infantry Division*
The 5th was a 'regular' division stationed before the war in the Catterick area of Northern Command, which explains the letter 'Y' for Yorkshire on its formation sign.

After the outbreak of war, its brigades were sent to France as independent infantry brigades in October 1939. Divisional headquarters followed them on 19 December and subsequently the division was reconstituted within the British Expeditionary Force.

On 23 March 1940, its 15th Brigade was sent to Norway and from there to Britain in May. The two remaining brigades, the 13th and 17th participated in the defence of Belgium and France against the German spring offensive. Under the command of Maj. General H. E. Franklyn these two brigades, two brigades of the 50th (Northumberland) Division and the 1st Army Tank Brigade formed 'Frankforce' which was deployed to defend the flank of the retreating BEF fighting at Ypres and on the Comines Canal.

After its return to Britain, the division served under Scottish Command, 3rd Corps and in Northern Ireland. At the beginning of May 1942, the 13th and 17th Brigades were shipped to Madagascar. The 15th Brigade left for India on 20 May, followed in June by the other two brigades, from Madagascar. During August and September 1942, the division moved to Iraq, later to Persia and Syria, and finally to Egypt in June 1943 to prepare for

13

Operation HUSKY. On 29 and 30 June, the 5th Division left Egypt on its way to Sicily.

## 5th Infantry Division

13th Infantry Brigade
  2nd The Cameronians (Scottish Rifles)
  2nd The Royal Inniskilling Fusiliers
  2nd The Wiltshire Regiment (Duke of Edinburgh's)
15th Infantry Brigade
  1st The Green Howards (Alexandra, Princess of Wales's Own Yorkshire Regiment)
  1st The King's Own Yorkshire Light Infantry
  1st The York and Lancaster Regiment
17th Infantry Brigade
  2nd The Royal Scots Fusiliers
  2nd The Northamptonshire Regiment
  6th Seaforth Highlanders (Ross-shire Buffs, The Duke of Albany's)

Divisional Troops
Royal Artillery
  91st, 92nd and 156th (Lanarkshire Yeomanry) Field Regiments
  52nd Anti-tank Regiment
  18th Light Anti-aircraft Regiment
Royal Engineers
  245th, 252nd and 38th Field Companies
  254th Field Park Companies
Royal Signals
  5th Division
Reconnaissance Corps
  5th Regiment (formerly 3rd Battalion The Tower Hamlets Rifles)
Machine-gun Battalion
  7th The Cheshire Regiment

### 50th (Northumbrian) Infantry Division

This was a first-line territorial division recruited from Northumberland and Durham as symbolised by the double 'T' in its formation sign, standing for the Tyne and Tees rivers.

The 50th Northumbrians embarked for France at the end of January 1940 as a 'motor' division with the 150th and 151st Brigades only. The division's third brigade, the 69th, was a second-line territorial brigade duplication of the 150th; it joined the 23rd Division of the BEF in April. The 50th Northumbrian

## Plate I

Three well-known leaders of the alliance are depicted in the plate's centre, accompanied by two of their soldiers, a British Army corporal of the 5th Infantry Division on the left and a US Army private on the right.

The corporal wears badges above his chevrons. At the bottom is the black flash of the Northamptonshire Regiment, which was part of the third brigade – the 17th – of the 5th Division, thence the three red strips below the divisional sign. The one, two, three red strips method to identify brigade seniority, was conceived in 1940 but as the composition of the divisions was later altered, the wearing of the strips lost its real significance (see Plate VIII, The Irish Brigade).

The Allied Forces Headquarters and the Mediterranean Allied Air Force were headquarters establishments. Their permanent staff wore a badge on the sleeves, the British on both, the Americans on the left sleeve only. The armlet was probably used by temporary staff. Both badges were used by the time of the landing in Sicily while the shoulder sleeve insignia of the 15th Army Group was adopted towards the end of the war.

Initially, the Allied Forces in Sicily included British, Americans, Canadians and a few French and Moroccans, but volunteers of many nationalities were part of the British Army and of the Royal Air Force. Volunteers from Newfoundland, for instance were in the latter, and manned the 166th (Newfoundland) Field Regiment, RA, of the British Army.

Prince Umberto of Savoy and an Italian general staff major of the Bersaglieri examine a map. The Prince wears grey-green uniform and the major wears the Italian khaki uniform, colonial pattern, with GS patches on the crimson Bersaglieri flames on the collar. *B. Montuori Collection*

Allied Forces Headquarters

Mediterranean Allied Air Force

Rhodesian Air Force

Canadian Air Force

Newfoundland

HQ AF

Headquarters Allied Forces

15th Army Group

New Zealand Air Force

2nd Polish Corps

Brazil

Division fought with the 5th Division, therefore earning the same battle honours, Ypres and Comines Canal, before withdrawing from Dunkirk.

In June 1940, the 50th was reorganised in Britain as an infantry division. In the summer of 1941, it was shipped to Egypt. Cyprus was its next station from August to November and then Iraq, less the 150th brigade which went to Palestine instead.

At the end of January 1942, the division arrived in the Western Desert where, on 3 June, the 150th Infantry Brigade was destroyed at Gazala and was never re-formed again. The two remaining brigades fought throughout that campaign from El Alamein to Tunisia and returned to Egypt in May 1943.

On 29 June 1943, the 50th (Northumbrian) Division embarked for Sicily.

**50th (Northumbrian) Infantry Division**

69th Infantry Brigade
  5th The East Yorkshire Regiment (The Duke of York's Own)
  6th and 7th The Green Howards (Alexandra, Princess of Wales's Own Yorkshire Regiment)
151st Infantry Brigade
  7th, 8th and 9th The Durham Light Infantry
168th (London) Infantry Brigade
  1st The London Scottish
  1st The London Irish Rifles
  10th The Royal Berkshire Regiment (Princess Charlotte of Wales's)

Divisional Troops
Royal Artillery
  74th, 124th and 90th Field Regiments
  102nd (Northumberland Hussars) Anti-tank Regiment

25th Light Anti-aircraft Regiment**
Royal Engineers
  233rd, 501st and 505th Field Companies
  235th Field Park Company
Royal Signals
  50 Division
Machine-gun Battalion
  2nd The Cheshire Regiment

*borrowed from 56th (London) Division at the end of May – see 56th Division.
**The 274th (Northumberland Hussars) LAA Battery was part of the 25th Light Anti-aircraft Regiment, RA

*51st (Highland) Infantry Division*

The 51st was a first-line territorial division composed of battalions of the Highland regiments, and was distinguished by the initials 'HD', for Highland Division, on the formation sign.

The 51st joined the BEF in France during January and February 1940 and was transferred to the French sector, on the Maginot Line, in April. As a result, the division became separated from the BEF by the German forces advancing from Belgium. The 154th Infantry Brigade and a number of small units formed 'Arkforce' with the task of defending the port of Le Havre from where a week later it was repatriated. The other two brigades became heavily engaged at Abbeville. Completely surrounded by the enemy, they surrendered on 12 June 1940.

Back in Britain, the 154th Brigade collected the men of the division who had escaped capture. By redesignating the 26th and 27th second line territorial brigades as the 152nd and 153rd

Brigades respectively, the division was brought back to its original strength.

In August 1942 the 51st division was back in action in Egypt and fought in every battle from El Alamein to Tunis. It assembled at Sousse before embarking for Sicily.

**51st (Highland) Infantry Division**

| | |
|---|---|
| 152nd Infantry Brigade | Divisional Troops |
|   2nd and 5th Seaforth Highlanders (Ross-shire Buffs, The Duke of Albany's) | Royal Artillery |
| |   126th, 127th and 128th Field Regiments |
|   5th The Queen's Own Cameron Highlanders |   61st Anti-tank Regiment |
| |   40th Light Anti-aircraft Regiment |
| 153rd Infantry Brigade | Royal Engineers |
|   1st and 5/7th The Gordon Highlanders |   274th, 275th and 276th Field Companies |
|   5th The Black Watch (Royal Highland Regiment) |   239th Field Park Company |
| 154th Infantry Brigade | Royal Signals |
|   1st and 7th The Black Watch (Royal Highland Regiment) |   51st Division |
| | Machine-gun Battalion |
|   7th The Argyll and Sutherland Highlanders (Princess Louise's) |   1/7th The Middlesex Regiment (The Duke of Cambridge's Own) |

*231st Infantry Brigade*

This was a regular infantry brigade stationed on the island of Malta and was therefore designated 1st (Malta) Infantry Brigade until 1 April 1943 when it was redesignated the 231st and became an independent formation. In honour of its service in Malta during the siege, its formation sign depicted a Maltese Cross on a scarlet shield.

**231st Infantry Brigade**

| | |
|---|---|
|   2nd The Devonshire Regiment | Royal Artillery |
|   1st The Dorsetshire Regiment |   165th Field Regiment |
|   1st The Hampshire Regiment |   300th Anti-tank Regiment |
| Brigade Troops |   352nd Light Anti-aircraft Regiment |
|   231st Infantry Brigade Support Company | Royal Engineers |
| |   66th Field Company |
| |   295th Field Company (from August 1943) |

*4th Armoured Brigade*

One of the first armoured formations to fight in the Western Desert, its original designation was the Heavy Armoured Group of the Mobile Division. In January 1940 it became the 7th Armoured Division and was redesignated the 4th Armoured Brigade.

It saw action throughout the North African Campaign until the surrender of the Axis Forces in Tunisia. The composition of the brigade was altered several times as it was often attached to different divisions although still part of the 7th armoured. In July 1942, it was re-formed as a light armoured brigade. On 1 June 1943, the title 'Light' was dropped as it was equipped with diesel Sherman tanks, in preparation for the invasion of Sicily.

17

Royal Navy Officers

Chief Petty Officer

Petty Officer

Miscellaneous
Junior Rating

Royal Air Force
Officers of Air Rank

Royal Air Force
Officers

Royal Air Force
Officers

Royal Canadian Air Force

Royal Australian
Air Force

South African
Air Force

Royal New Zealand
Air Force

R.N. COMMANDO

Royal Navy Commando

Royal Air
Force Officers
Forage Cap

Warrant Officers

US Navy
Officers

US Navy
Petty Officers

The Welch Regiment

Beach Groups

The Highland Light Infantry
(City of Glasgow Regiment)

THE HAMPSHIRE REGT

The Hampshire Regiment

**Plate II**
The Royal Navy, the US Navy, the Royal Air Force and the US Army Air Forces were fully engaged in the landing operations in Sicily and throughout the Italian campaign until the end of the war. Admiral Sir Andrew Cunningham and Air Marshal Sir Arthur Tedder were the sea and air commanders, respectively

The American air force was not yet independent from the army and therefore used army uniforms and insignia, but with the winged propeller on the collar.

Some British Commonwealth contingents were part of the Mediterranean Air Command. The officers wore RAF cap badges and cloth shoulder titles which identified their nationality – light blue on grey-blue – while airmen had different cap badges as well as shoulder titles – light blue on black, or dark blue. Red on khaki titles were used on khaki drill jackets. The Commonwealth air forces' cap badges are shown in this plate and examples of shoulder titles in the previous plate.

The Beach Group was an essential component of sea landing forces. It organised the initial landing, defended the beach-head and supervised the flow of reinforcements and supplies on the beach-head. Several infantry battalions were attached to Beach Groups, the 2/4th Hampshires and the 1st Welch, for instance, were among the first units to land in Sicily.

By July 1943, the brigade was composed of the following units:

**4th Armoured Brigade**

'A' Squadron 1st The Royal Dragoons
3rd County of London Yeomanry (Sharpshooters)
44th Royal Tank Regiment
2nd The King's Royal Rifle Corps

Brigade Troops
5th Company, RASC
14th Light Field Ambulance
318th Armoured Brigade Workshop, REME

*23rd Armoured Brigade*

This brigade was formed on 1 November 1940 from the 23rd Army Tank Brigade. It was re-organised as an independent armoured brigade group on 12 July 1942, after its arrival in Egypt. It took part in all operations on the Alamein Line and in Tunisia at Medenine, on the Mareth Line, at Akarit and at Enfidaville.

**23rd Armoured Brigade**

40th, 46th and 50th Royal Tank Regiments
11th The King's Royal Rifle Corps (Queen's Westminsters)

Brigade Troops
331st Company RASC
150th Light Field Ambulance

*78th Infantry Division*

The 'Battle-axe' division was formed in Scotland in June 1942 by the 1st (Guards), 11th and 36th Infantry Brigades and support units drawn from various sources. After a period of training, the division left the Clyde for North Africa on 27 October 1942. Spearheaded by the 11th Brigade, the division landed on 8 November, in Algeria, with the US 34th Infantry Division. Bitter fighting followed at the Tebourba Gap in December and throughout the winter of 1942–43 in Algeria and Tunisia.

After the end of the hostilities in Africa, the 78th Division became part of 8th Army's reserve. In July 1943, it was composed of the following units:

**78th Infantry Division**

11th Infantry Brigade
2nd The Lancashire Fusiliers
1st The East Surrey Regiment
5th The Northamptonshire Regiment
36th Infantry Brigade
6th The Queen's Own Royal West Kent Regiment
5th The Buffs (Royal East Kent Regt)
8th The Argyll and Sutherland Highlanders (Princess Louise's)
38th (Irish) Infantry Brigade
2nd The London Irish Rifles
1st The Royal Irish Fusiliers (Princess Victoria's)
6th The Royal Inniskilling Fusiliers

Divisional Troops
Royal Artillery
17th, 132nd (Glamorgan Yeomanry) and 138th Field Regiments
64th (The Queen's Own Royal Glasgow Yeomanry) Anti-tank Regiments
49th Light Anti-aircraft Regiment
Royal Engineers
214th, 237th and 256th Field Companies
281st Field Park Company
Royal Signals
78th Division
Reconnaissance Corps
56th Regiment (formerly The Artists Rifle)
Machine-gun Battalion
1st Princess Louise's Kensington Regiment

19

## 43rd Infantry Brigade

This brigade's headquarters was formed in the United Kingdom in August 1943 and was sent to Tunisia in the following month for security duties on the lines of communications of the Allied Forces HQ. All its component battalions were numbered '30th', and manned by personnel mainly below category 'A'.

Three battalions were sent to Sicily on 5 November 1943. For deception purposes, each battalion was designated brigade, the 119th, 120th and 121st, respectively, and the brigade was redesignated Headquarters 40th Division.

Having served its purpose, the brigade HQ was disbanded in Sicily at the end of June 1944.

**43rd Infantry Brigade**
30th The Somerset Light Infantry
  (Prince Albert's)
30th The Royal Norfolk Regiment
30th The Dorset Regiment

## British 8th Army – Special Forces

### The Commandos

The British World War Two airborne forces, commandos and Special Air Service have common origins, due to the similarity of their training, skills and roles. The army commandos were instituted in June 1940. On the night of the 23rd/24th of that month, scarcely three weeks after the idea of raising such a force had been conceived, No 11 Commando (a fictitious designation at that time) sailed for France on its first experimental mission.

It was initially decided to form ten commandos each consisting of ten troops of fifty men, but their composition was changed in 1941 to six troops of sixty-five men.

Nos 1 and 2 Commandos were to have been airborne units. After the first contingent of volunteers on parachute training were absorbed in the airborne establishment (it formed eventually the 1st Parachute Battalion), the project was abandoned and the recruits were trained mainly as seaborne assault troops.

In June 1940, Sir D. W. Cameron of Lochiel, the Chief of the Clan Cameron of Scotland gave hospitality to No 1 Independent Commando Company in his castle at Achnacarry, near Fort William. In December 1940, the castle and its grounds became the location of the commando special training centre. Twelve months later, the depot was established at Achnacarry. About 25,000 recruits were trained there, including US Army Rangers and the foreign recruits who joined No 10 (Inter-Allied) Commando.

Twelve commandos were formed in a short time and were placed under the supervision of the Special Service Brigade.

The commandos were constantly engaged in raiding missions along the Norwegian and French coasts, on the Lofoten Islands, at Vaagso, Spitzbergen, St Nazaire and Dieppe, to mention just some of their best known raids.

In February 1941, Nos 7, 8 and 11 Commandos were trans-

The worst news that a family in Britain could hear about a loved one. Private Cecil Humphrey's unit had just been relieved from the front line on the Garigliano when they heard German mortar fire hitting their former positions. A group of them decided to go back to lend a hand – Humphrey was killed.

No. Cas/ 65/ 12441
(If replying, please quote above No.)

Army Form B. 104—82.

Infantry　　　　Record Office,
ASHFORD, Middlesex.

25th February 1944.

Madam,

It is my painful duty to inform you that a report has been received from the War Office notifying the death of :—

(No.) 6106632　　　(Rank)　Private

(Name)　Cecil Reginald HUMPHREY

(Regiment)　The Queen's Royal Regiment

which occurred　in the Central Mediterranean Theatre of War

on the　26th January, 1944.

The report is to the effect that he was killed in Action

I am to express the sympathy and regret of the Army Council.

I am to add that any information that may be received as to the soldier's burial will be communicated to you in due course.

I am,

Mrs. N.M. Humphrey,
L. Evelyn Cottages,
South Godstone, Surrey.

Madam,
Your obedient Servant,

Major
for Officer in Charge of Records.

JP [76028] 30253/— 500m 9/39 M&C Ltd. 706 Forms/B.104—82/6
[P.T.O.

ferred to the Middle East under the command of Lt Colonel R. E. Laycock and became known there as 'Layforce'. The raids on Bardia and on Rommel's headquarters are well remembered together with the exploits of No 11 Commando on the Litani River in Syria. Commandos fought at Tobruk during the first siege and on Crete to cover the withdrawal of the British garrison. Layforce had to be disbanded due to excessive casualties and Lt Colonel Laycock returned to Britain in December 1941 to take over command of the Special Service Brigade.

In February 1942, the Royal Marines raised their first two commando units, designated Nos 40 and 41 (Royal Marine) Commandos. Eight RM commandos were formed before the end of the war.

As the war progressed in favour of the Allies, the commandos became invaluable in the role of spearhead for landing armies. No 5 Commando was deployed in this role during the invasion of Madagascar in May 1942. In November 1942, Nos 1 and 6 Commandos landed in North Africa and later fought in Tunisia as part of the field army.

Three commandos were designated to aid the 8th Army's landing in Sicily: No 3 Commando, and Nos 40 and 41 (RM) Commandos. The first two had previously suffered severe casualties at Dieppe. No 3 Commando was reinforced by recruits from the civil police. After a period of training at Weymouth, it was shipped to Gibraltar, then Algiers in April 1943, and from thence to Alexandria, via Sfax, where it was attached to 13th Corps, in readiness for Operation HUSKY. The RM commandos were transferred from the Isle of Wight to Scotland for a spell of training before embarking on the voyage towards Sicily on 28 June 1943.

No 2 Commando replaced No 3 Commando at Gibraltar. As four commandos were in the same operational area, they were grouped into a brigade under its own headquarters under the command of Laycock.

*The 1st Airborne Division*
In November 1940, No 2 Commando was redesignated 11th Special Air Service Battalion, which consisted of a Parachute Wing and a Glider Wing. In September 1941, it was renamed 1st Parachute Battalion.

The battalion was ordered to Hardwick, Derbyshire. There, the 1st Parachute Brigade was to be formed with four battalions. In February 1942, the brigade's parachute battalions became part of the Parachute Regiment and its glider battalions became part of the Glider Pilot Regiment. The two regiments constituted the Army Air Corps, whose cap badge they wore.

The first distinction of the paratroopers was the lanyard, green for the 1st, yellow for the 2nd, red for the 3rd and black for the 4th Parachute Battalion. The red beret was adopted when the brigade was at Bulford, on Salisbury Plain, and was worn for the first time in North Africa, in November 1942. The distinctive winged cap badge was authorised in May 1943 for all ranks of the Parachute Regiment, and thus the previous badge remained confined to the personnel of the Army Air Corps.

On 31 July 1942, the 4th battalion left the 1st Parachute Brigade and became part of the 2nd Parachute Brigade together with the 5th (Scottish) Parachute Battalions and the 6th (Royal Welch) Parachute Battalion.

The 5th Battalion was officially designated 'Scottish' because it was recruited primarily from a battalion of the Queen's Own Cameron Highlanders and later from other Scottish battalions. Therefore, in accordance with tradition, the men wore the Balmoral bonnet with the Army Air Corps badge on a Hunting Stuart tartan patch until September 1944, when they opted for the red beret.

The men of the 6th Battalion were Welsh as recruiting started within the 10th Royal Welch Fusiliers. Therefore, all ranks wore the black flash of the Royal Welch Fusiliers.

The headquarters of the 4th Parachute Brigade was formed in

**Plate III**
The review of the campaign's leaders continues with Lt General Carl Spaatz, in command of the United States Army Air Forces, and General Sir Bernard L. Montgomery, the 8th Army's commander.

The former, seen searching for his lighter, was wearing the service uniform with cap and jacket of dark shade, and grey trousers. Several patterns of dark shade jackets existed, long and short (see Plate XXII) and the latter was generally known as the 'Ike jacket' because General Eisenhower put it in fashion and it was in fact adopted for all ranks in October 1944 in olive drab (khaki). General Montgomery was wearing his usual beret with two badges and light khaki uniform.

Four main types of badges were worn in the British Army: the cap badge, the formation sign, the cloth shoulder title and the arm-of-service strip. Some regiments also used regimental flashes. Formation signs were adopted during World War One and identified brigades, divisions and higher formations. Cloth shoulder titles replaced metal ones in World War Two from 1940. Arm-of-service strips were also introduced in 1940, for all ranks, for wearing on each sleeve of the battledress blouse below the formation sign.

Officers were instructed to wear their stars and crowns worsted on coloured felt, the colours of which varied according to arm or corps.

ROYAL ARTILLERY

Field Marshal

Brigadier and Substantive Colonel

Generals

ROYAL ENGINEERS

Royal Regiment of Artillery

Corps of Royal Engineers

Infantry
(except Rifle regiments)

Rifle Regiments

13th CORPS

8th ARMY

30th CORPS

ROYAL ARMOURED CORPS

Royal Armoured Corps

RECONNAISSANCE

1st King's Dragoon
Guards

Reconnaissance Corps

1st The Royal Dragoons

the Middle East on 1 December 1942. The 10th Parachute Battalion was raised initially from volunteers from the Royal Sussex Regiment and trained in Palestine where it was joined by the 156th Battalion, from India. The 156th Battalion was formed from volunteers from various British Army regiments in India on 18 October 1941 as the 151st Parachute Battalion and was renumbered on joining the brigade in the Middle East. The 11th Parachute Battalion was formed from a nucleus of officers and men from the 156th, thus completing the order of battle of the 1st Airborne Division.

The 1st Parachute Brigade had fought in North Africa since November 1942, winning nine battle honours – Soudia, Oudna, Djebel Azzag, Djebel Alliliga, El Hadjeba, Tamera, Djebel Dahra, Kef el Debna and North Africa 1942–43 – with the loss of 1,700 men killed, wounded and missing.

After the end of the hostilities in Tunisia on 9 May 1943, the brigade was sent to regroup and train near Mascara, about 60 miles south-east of Oran. There, it was joined by the 2nd Parachute Brigade on 23 April and by the 1st Airlanding Brigade on 26 May 1943, both from the United Kingdom.

Another two parachute battalions, the 10th and the 156th, joined the 1st Airborne Division in June as part of the 4th Parachute Brigade. The 11th Parachute Battalion was formed by a nucleus of men from the 156th and was the last to join the division in North Africa.

The composition of the British airborne forces earmarked for the invasion of Sicily was as follows:

**1st Airborne Division**

1st Parachute Brigade
  1st, 2nd and 3rd Parachute Battalions
2nd Parachute Brigade
  4th, 5th (Scottish) and 6th (Royal Welch) Parachute Battalions
4th Parachute Brigade
  10th, 11th and 156th Parachute Battalions
1st Airlanding Brigade
  1st The Border Regiment
  2nd The South Staffordshire Regiment
Divisional Troops
  Royal Artillery
  1st Airlanding Light Regiment

1st and 2nd Airlanding Anti-tank Batteries
1st Airlanding Light Anti-aircraft Battery
Royal Engineers
  9th Field Company
  261st Field Park Company
  1st, 2nd and 4th Parachute Squadrons
Royal Signals
  1st Airborne Division
Reconnaissance Corps
  1st Airlanding Squadron
Army Air Corps
  21st Independent Parachute Company

Before the end of June, the 1st and 2nd Parachute Brigades were moved to a new training camp near Sousse, in Tunisia, in readiness for the MARSTON Operation.

*The Special Air Service*

The Special Air Service was raised by Lt Colonel David Stirling, in July 1941, as a para-commando unit to be deployed to sabotage the lines of communications of the Axis forces.

Maj. General Anders with Polish and Italian officers. Behind him two Italian officers wear the old grey-green Italian uniform with rank insignia on the cuffs and the Savoy shield of the 1st Motorised Group on the left breast. The artillery lieutenant still wears the collar patches of the 11th Field Artillery, 'Mantova' Division. The infantry lieutenant shaking hands with the general wears khaki uniform, colonial pattern, without the Savoy shield. The Polish captain in the foreground wears British battledress and the badge of the Independent Carpathian Rifle Brigade on the left breast pocket, as a veteran of the Western Desert Campaign. *Polish Institute and Sikorski Museum Collection*

The first recruits came from 'Layforce' and training on parachuting and demolition began at Kibrit, Egypt. Subsequently, several missions were accomplished behind the enemy line, often in co-operation with the Long Range Desert Group, another independent force, whose role was mainly reconnaissance. Parachute missions were abandoned in favour of infiltration on land, through the desert, behind the enemy lines, which cost the Axis about 300 aircraft destroyed on the ground, not to mention the losses inflicted by the many attacks on convoys, railways and various military installations.

In January 1943, the 1st Special Air Service was formed on a cadre of five squadrons. In the meantime, a branch of the force had specialised in naval warfare, operating on small boats in the Aegean.

Lt Colonel Stirling was captured by the enemy near El Hamma, in southern Tunisia. As a consequence, the SAS was split up into two units, the Special Raiding Squadron in charge of land operations under the command of Lt Colonel R. B. (Paddy) Mayne and the Special Boat Section, later Special Boat Service, under Lt Colonel Lord Jellicoe.

The 2nd Special Air Service was raised in the sector of 1st Army and its command was taken by Lt Colonel William Stirling, David's brother. A training camp was established near Philippeville, Algeria, where nearby were camped Lord Jellicoe's SBS and 'Popski's Private Army'.

A squadron of 2nd SAS was given the task of spearheading the landing of the 51st (Highland) Division on Sicily and was transferred to Sousse in due time.

### Beach Groups
The task of a Beach Group was to assist the landing of men, vehicles and stores over open beaches in the early stages of a seaborne invasion of enemy territory before the capture or

**R.A.S.C.**

Royal Army
Service Corps

Royal Army
Ordnance Corps

**ROYAL SIGNALS**

Royal Corps of Signals

Corps of Military
Police

**R.A.M.C.**

Royal Army Medical
Corps

Royal Army
Veterinary Corps

Royal Army
Pay Corps

**R.E.M.E.**

Royal Electrical and
Mechanical Engineers

Army Educational
Corps

Military Provost Staff
Corps

Army Dental
Corps

Intelligence Corps

Royal Army Chaplains
Department
(Christian and Jewish)

Army Catering
Corps

Pioneer Corps

Army Territorial
Service

Entertainments
National
Services
Association

Navy, Army
and Air Force
Institute

Army Physical Training
Corps

General Service Corps

**Plate IV**
The badges of the British Army supporting corps are displayed in this plate along with those of the Navy, Army and Air Force Institutions (NAAFI) and of the Entertainment National Service Association (ENSA), which surely both deserve a credit.

The Army Council Instructions of 18 September 1940 introduced the arm-of-service strips, with amendments dated 27 December 1941, and the former introduced coloured cloth shoulder titles for the foot guards (see Plate XXV) and coloured backing to the officers' rank insignia, but coloured cloth shoulder titles for the whole British Army were adopted in June 1943. A few examples in printed and embroidered variations are illustrated and all the cap badges with their arm-of-service strips below. The strips were 2 inches by ¼ inch in size and were made of felt, or were embroidered or printed.

Corporal Harold B. Stokes of the 209th Company RASC, on the left, was at that time on a trip to Rome, probably late in the war, because he wore the general service cap, i.e. the khaki beret, adopted in September 1943. On the sleeves he had the rhinoceros of the 1st Armoured Division, the arm-of-service strip but no shoulder title.

The machine gunner, on the other side, is pictured in a battle action and therefore did not wear any unit or formation badge.

construction of adequate ports, and to protect the beaches from enemy land, sea or air counter-attacks.

Two Beach Groups depended from a Beach Sub-area which had the capability of landing two divisions in the first forty-eight hours.

A Beach Group contained a variety of troops, an infantry battalion being the prevalent component. The first parties to land were detachments of Royal Navy commandos and beach companies which marked suitable landing spots and beach limits and chose suitable exits from the beach, which were bulldozed by the sappers. Beach roadways were laid (Somerfeld track) to the nearest main lateral road. Locations for headquarters, field dressing stations and dumps were established, and the provost erected traffic signs. Beach recovery sections started to recover sunk or damaged vehicles which were removed to a Drowned Vehicle Park where REME personnel repaired them.

Meanwhile, the group commander led reconnaissance parties inland in order to assess the situation because the first priority was that units could move inland immediately after landing.

RAF commandos had the task of either capturing or establishing airfields.

## US 7th Army
### 1st Infantry Division 'Fighting First'
This Regular Army division derived from the 1st Expeditionary Division which went to the Western Front during World War One. There it achieved a number of records: the first US Army division to arrive in France; the first on the front; the first to suffer casualties; and the first to be cited in general orders. Later, it was the first US Army Division to enter Germany.

Its insignia, a red figure '1' adopted on 31 October 1918, was the origin of the division's second nickname 'The Red One'.

From March to August 1942, the 1st Division completed training at Camp Blanding, Florida, and Indiantown Gap, Pennsylvania. It then sailed for the United Kingdom to become part of the Centre Task Force, preparing for the invasion of North Africa.

On 8 November 1942, the division landed near Oran which it surrounded to prevent the arrival of Vichy French reinforcements. It was in action on the following day when the Vichy forces attacked. After the cease fire declared by Admiral Darlan, the division moved against the real enemy, the Axis Forces, and fought in North Africa throughout that campaign.

**1st Infantry Division 'Fighting First'**
1st, 18th and 26th Infantry Regiment
5th, 7th, 32nd and 33rd Field Artillery Battalions
1st Engineers Battalion
1st Medical Battalion
1st Signal Company
701st Ordnance Company
1st Quartermaster Company
1st Reconnaissance Troop

### 3rd Infantry Division 'Marne'

The three white stripes on the shoulder sleeve insignia of this Regular Army division refer to the three major operations in which it participated during World War One on the Marne river, in France.

After the postwar demobilisation, the 3rd was one of the four divisions maintained in operational order at Camp Lewis, Washington. After being moved to Camp Pickett, Virginia, in September 1943, it became part of the Western Task Force due to land in Western Morocco directly from the United States. The 3rd Division landed at Fedhala, north of Casablanca, against strong opposition from French naval batteries and ground forces. Later, the division took part in the fighting for Tunisia.

**3rd Infantry Division 'Marne'**

| | |
|---|---|
| 7th, 15th and 30th Infantry Regiments | 3rd Medical Battalion |
| 9th, 10th, 39th and 41st Field Artillery Battalions | 3rd Signal Company |
| | 703rd Ordnance Company |
| 10th Engineers Battalion | 3rd Quartermaster Company |
| | 3rd Reconnaissance Troop |

### 9th Infantry Division

The 9th was the last among the nine Regular Army divisions organised in 1920 but lost all its units during the following years.

The division was reorganised in August 1940 at Fort Bragg, North Carolina. It was assigned to the Western Task Force of the North African invasion forces, although its 39th Regimental Combat Team was sent to the United Kingdom to join the Centre Task Force.

During the invasion of North Africa, the 9th Infantry Division landed at Mehdia in the northern sector, together with the 2nd Armoured Division. Their objective was the capture of an airfield which was secured after two days of fighting. Later, it participated in the North African campaign and in major engagements at El Guettar and Bizerte.

**9th Infantry Division**

| | |
|---|---|
| 39th, 47th and 60th Infantry Regiment | 9th Medical Battalion |
| 26th, 34th, 60th and 84th Field Artillery Battalions | 9th Signal Company |
| | 709th Ordnance Company |
| 15th Engineers Battalion | 9th Quartermaster Company |
| | 9th Reconnaissance Troop |

### 45th Infantry Division 'Thunderbird'

This division, which traces its origin to the Oklahoma Militia, was created by the National Defense Act of 1920 as a National Guard division from among four states, Oklahoma, Colorado, Arizona and New Mexico.

In August 1940, the 45th Division was ordered into Federal service for a one-year training program at Fort Sill, Oklahoma, but the United States entered World War Two before the end of its training. The division was transferred to Texas, Louisiana, at

Benjamin Spreadbury and Angus McLeod, RAF Regiment, in a photograph taken in Naples before Montecassino was captured in the spring of 1944. Both wear the ribbon of the Africa Star and Angus McLeod wears the three years' Good Conduct Service chevrons on his forearms. *B. Spreadbury Collection*

Camp Edwards, Massachusetts, where it was trained for amphibious operations, with further amphibious training following at Camp Pickett, Vermont.

In June 1943, the division was sent to North Africa in readiness for the invasion of Sicily.

### 45th Infantry Division
**'Thunderbird'**

| | |
|---|---|
| 157th, 179th and 180th Infantry Regiments | 120th Medical Battalion |
| 158th, 160th, 171st and 189th Field Artillery Battalions | 45th Signal Company |
| | 700th Ordnance Company |
| 120th Engineers Battalion | 45th Quartermaster Company |
| | 45th Reconnaissance Troop |

### 2nd Armored Division 'Hell on Wheels'

The initial training of the 2nd Armored was undertaken at Fort Benning, Georgia, where it was activated in June 1940. The division participated in the Tennessee, Louisiana and Carolina manoeuvres in 1941. In August 1942, it had special training on the Carolina coast under Atlantic Fleet Amphibious Force.

As part of the Western Task Force for the invasion of North Africa, the 2nd Armored Division landed in the northern sector, near Mehdia, in Western Morocco and later fought in Tunisia.

### 2nd Armored Division
**'Hell on Wheels'**

| | |
|---|---|
| 63rd and 67th Armored Regiment | 45th Armored Medical Battalion |
| 41st Armored Infantry Regiment | 3rd Armored Ordnance Company |
| 54th, 67th and 391st Armored Field Artillery Battalions | 143rd Armored Signals Company |
| | 83rd Armored Reconnaissance Troop |
| 23rd Armored Engineers Battalion | |

### 82nd Airborne Division 'All American'

Composed of men from Georgia, Alabama and Tennessee, this was an infantry division first raised in 1917. During training most of its personnel went to other divisions and replacements came from all over the United States making it an 'All American' outfit. In France, Corporal Alvin C. York of the 82nd Division distinguished himself by shooting fifteen and capturing 132 Germans single-handedly in one action. The division was disbanded in 1919.

The 'All American' was reactivated on 25 March 1942 at Camp Claiborne, Louisiana, under the command of Maj.General Omar N. Bradley who, in June, was replaced by Maj.General Matthew B. Ridgway. Under Ridgway's leadership the 82nd was reorganised and trained in the airborne role at Claiborne and later at Fort Bragg, North Carolina. Early in 1943, the division was moved to New England where it embarked for North Africa. After a couple of months spent training in the area of Oujda-Marhnia the 82nd Division was moved to Kairoun on the eve of D-Day, Sicily.

**82nd Airborne Division**
**'All American'**

| | |
|---|---|
| 325th Glider Infantry Regiment | 80th Anti-aircraft Battalion |
| 504th and 505th Parachute Infantry Regiment | 307th Airborne Engineers Battalion |
| | 307th Airborne Medical Company |
| 319th and 320th Glider Field Artillery Battalion | 82nd Airborne Signal Company |
| | 782nd Airborne Ordnance Company |
| 376th and 456th Parachute Field Artillery Battalion | 407th Airborne Quartermaster Company |

A unit linked with the 82nd Airborne Division was the 509th Parachute Infantry Battalion which at that time was also in North Africa. It was originally the 2nd Battalion of the 503rd Regiment which had been sent to Britain in 1942 to join the British airborne establishment. It was redesignated 509th Parachute Infantry Battalion, went to North Africa with the invading forces and made the first two American combat jumps, at Lourmel in Morocco and at Youks Les Bains in Algeria.

*Rangers*

The 1st Ranger Battalion was constituted on 27 May 1942 and activated on 19 June at Carrickfergus, Northern Ireland, with personnel from units in US Army Northern Ireland Forces (USANIF) under the command of Major William O. Darby. This unit landed in North Africa on 8 November 1942 and took part in the subsequent campaign, fighting with special distinction at El Guettar.

The 3rd and 4th Ranger Battalions were raised in North Africa on 25 May and 8 June 1943, respectively. On 1 August, the three battalions in existence were redesignated 1st, 2nd and 3rd Ranger Infantry Battalion.

The three battalions spearheaded the US 7th Army landing in Sicily. They later landed at Salerno and Anzio. Although the 2nd and 3rd battalions were virtually wiped out near Cisterna, the remaining troops participated in the advance from Rome to the Arno river. During that campaign the Rangers were sent back to the United States where the 1st and 3rd Battalions were disbanded on 15 August 1944 and the 4th Battalion on 24 October. William O. Darby returned to Italy and was killed in action in the Po valley on 10 April 1945.

## THE ALLIED MILITARY GOVERNMENT OF THE OCCUPIED TERRITORY

Before the invasion of Sicily, the Allies were confronted by the problem of how to administer an enemy territory. In Africa, the British military authorities had organised the administration of the ex-Italian colonies; the French continued to administer their own territories. Obviously, however, the Allies could not replace the whole existing Fascist civil administration in Sicily. Therefore, the Allied Forces Headquarters decided to form a new organisation manned by

**Plate V**

The badges of the 1st Airborne Division, of the Army and Royal Marine Commandos and of other British elite units are displayed on this plate. Most of these formations and units were in Sicily, but some joined in the Italian campaign later.

The paratroopers wore the cap badge of the Parachute Regiment and, on the sleeves, their own shoulder title and the Pegasus badge. The glider pilots had the cap badge of the Army Air Corps. The troops of the glider-borne battalions and of the support corps and services continued wearing their own cap badges but on the red beret. Airborne troops, apart from the Parachute Regiment who already had a shoulder title, wore the straight 'Airborne' title under the Pegasus badge; those who did not, wore the curved 'Airborne' title above the Pegasus badge. However, it is difficult to set a strict rule on the wearing of these badges because not all units conformed. Often, they simply could not obtain a newly-adopted insignia.

The Commandos wore the shoulder title above the Combined Operations badge. They had a green beret. The Royal Marines had their cap badge, while the Army Commandos as a rule had no badge, although a special cap badge for No 2 Commando was adopted in 1942.

Illustrated in the centre are an NCO of the RASC, a Bren gunner of the 1st Airborne Division, and a commando wearing the Denison smock and denim trousers.

No2 Commando

No3 Commando

The Parachute Regiment

Army Air Corps

Combined Operations

Nos 40 and 41 (Royal Marines) Commando

2nd Battalion
The South Staffordshire Regiment

1st Battalion The Border Regiment

Airborne Troops other than
Parachute Regiment

Qualified Parachutist

Special Air Service
Regiment

Long Range Desert
Group

Raiding Support
Regiment

specialists in civil affairs, capable of supervising temporarily the Italian civil administration until a free election could be held in Italy.

The Allied Military Government of Occupied Territory (AMGOT) was created officially on 1 May 1943 as a mixed American and British organisation with the task of establishing its own officials in every major Italian town to supervise the activities of the local administrations. The AMGOT comprised six branches, Legal, Financial, Civilian Supply, Public Health, Public Safety and the Allied and Enemy Property Division, staffed by officials with various appointments, headed by General Alexander who was the Military Governor of Sicily.

The fall of the Fascist Government on 25 July 1943 aided considerably the work of the AMGOT but, throughout the war, AMGOT and the field commands never managed to establish either a common purpose or reciprocal co-operation.

## THE CAMPAIGN OF SICILY

### British 8th Army

After landing in the south-east corner of Sicily on 10 July 1943, and consolidating the beachheads, the 8th Army's objective was to drive hard north up the island's east coast to reach and bypass the city of Catania as soon as possible before the Axis forces could set up a defensive line around Mount Etna. Therefore, to facilitate a speedy advance along the coastal road, a series of operations (Operation MARSTON) was planned in order to secure the main bridges on the way to Catania.

The first phase of the plan contemplated the capture of three bridges. The 1st Airlanding Brigade was to capture a bridge south of Syracuse, Ponte Grande over the Anapo river, by a glider-borne assault which was part of the initial landing, going in on 10 July 1943. Later, on the night of 13 July, a parachute landing south of Augusta by the 2nd Parachute Brigade and a commando raid would be made, aimed at the capture the Ponte dei Malati, on the River San Leonardo. Finally, the same night, the 1st Parachute Brigade was entrusted with the capture of Primosole Bridge over the River Simeto, south of Catania.

Perhaps the plan could have been successful and Etna could have been bypassed earlier if a gale had not jeopardised the initial landings.

### Airborne Landings

The 1st Airlanding Brigade left Tunisia in the later afternoon of 9 July in 137 Waco gliders towed by C-47s.

Eight Horsa gliders carried support weapons and stores. Before they reached Malta the wind grew into a gale. After a three-hour flight the pilots were having difficulties controlling the storm-tossed gliders. As the formation approached the Sicilian coast, streams of tracer came up and explosive shells burst in the darkness. Many gliders were released too soon and crash landed in the sea.

Contrary to expectation, there was little or no moonlight and the land was enveloped in clouds of dust which impaired visibility. As a result, only fifty-two gliders made it to the land. Most of the others fell into the sea. Twenty-five gliders were never seen or heard of again, and 252 men were drowned.

Only twelve gliders landed in the vicinity of the main target. Ponte Grande was captured by a party of fourteen South Staffords, later reinforced by seventy men, some of them from the Border Regiment. It was held for fourteen hours against ever increasing counter-attacks until the afternoon of 10 July. Fortunately, half an hour later, the bridge was recaptured by troops of the 17th Infantry Brigade before the enemy had time to blow it up.

### Commando Landings

Nos 40 and 41 (Royal Marine) Commandos were to land in the 1st Canadian Division's area with the task of destroying some coastal defence batteries while No 3 Commando's task was to silence a battery located about three miles inland, near the town of Cassabile, and to secure the beach near Scoglio Imbiancato.

As the weather deteriorated on 9 July a strong wind and rough sea caught the assaulting fleet approaching the beaches. When the wind suddenly abated, all units started to transfer into the landing craft. The landing craft of No 40 Commando became mingled with the Canadian boats, which they should have preceded. Both Nos 40 and 41 Commandos landed on the wrong beaches, No 41 at 0300 hours, half an hour late. Nevertheless, they achieved their objective of destroying the Italian batteries, which turned out to be machine-gun positions.

The landing craft carrying No 3 Commando left the convoy at 0130 hours and the commandos carried out their tasks as planned, almost without loss.

### SAS Objectives

The objective of 2nd Special Air Service was the capture of a lighthouse on the extremity of Capo Passero, in the middle of the 51st (Highland) Division's landing area, which was believed to be defended by a number of machine-guns.

However, during the first few days in Tunisia the raiding party was affected by malaria and thirty-two of its forty-five men became sick. The remainder of the party landed and captured the lighthouse before dawn on 10 July without a shot being fired, as the objective was defended by a single machine-gun and three soldiers.

### Land Army

On landing, the 8th Army comprised 13th Corps with the 5th and the 50th Infantry Divisions and 30th Corps with the 1st Canadian and the 51st (Highland) Infantry Divisions, and the 231st Infantry Brigade.

The 4th Armoured Brigade and the 23rd Independent Armoured Brigade Group were attached to 13th and 30th Corps,

Private G. Cori wearing British Army battledress with Italian insignia. The stars on the collar were and still are the main emblem of the Italian armed forces. He wears the 'Italy' shoulder title above the green, white and red strip on the upper sleeve. Cori was probably an ex POW in Britain, who opted to join the King's Army in Italy.
*A. Stevens Collection*

33

CANADA

1st CANADIAN INFANTRY DIVISION

THE ROYAL CANADIAN REGIMENT

The Royal Canadian Regiment

The Hastings and
Prince Edward Regiment

48th Highlanders
of Canada

Royal 22ᵉ Régiment

The Carlton and
York Regiment

Princess Patricia's
Canadian Light Infantry

The Seaforth Highlanders
of Canada

The Edmonton Regiment

WEST.NOVA-SCOTIA.REGT.

The West Nova
Scotia Regiment

The Royal Canadian
Dragoons

The Saskatoon
Light Infantry

Corps of Royal
Canadian Engineers

Royal Canadian
Corps of Signals

Royal Canadian
Army Service Corps

Royal Canadian
Army Medical
Corps

Canadian
Dental Corps

Canadian
Provost Corps

Royal Canadian
Ordnance Corps

Corps of Royal
Canadian Electrical
and Mechanical Engineers

**Plate VI**
Although the British troops landed in Sicily wearing long trousers, photographic evidence suggests that the Canadians wore shorts, including Maj. General Guy G. Simonds, commanding the 1st Canadian Infantry Division, here seen wading ashore from a landing craft. While the general wears the conventional 'Bombay Bloomers' or a similar style of trousers, the lance corporal on the right had his shortened.

Another peculiarity of the Canadians at that time was that many units wore the formation sign and the cloth shoulder title on the sleeves of the khaki drill shirt, possibly because some shirts do not seem to have shoulder straps. British troops had the formation sign on 'slip-ons' on the shoulder straps or, later, sewn on a patch which was attached to the outer ends of these.

The average head-dress was the khaki field service cap, with exceptions for corps and regiments that were entitled to wear a special head-dress. The general, for instance, is shown wearing the black beret of the armoured forces, with general's cap badge.

This plate also displays all the cap badges and a small selection of cloth shoulder titles of the 1st Canadian Infantry Division, the divisional formation sign, and the cap badges of the supporting corps.

respectively, as tank support formations. The component units of the 4th Armoured Brigade, for instance, were assigned as follows: the 3rd County of London Yeomanry was placed under command of the 5th Division and the 44th Royal Tanks under the 50th; tactical brigade headquarters was to accompany HQ 13th Corps on the invasion, with the rest of the headquarters following on D+28; and the 2nd The King's Royal Rifle Corps remained temporarily at Tripoli.

The landings and subsequent operations on Saturday, 10 July, proceeded according to plan and, although the actual landing and regrouping of the units took longer than was envisaged, Syracuse was entered within the same day. The planned landing of the 2nd Parachute Brigade near Augusta was therefore cancelled, and the town was captured during the night of 12 July.

During the following day, 13 July, the commander and staff of the Italian 54th 'Napoli' Division surrendered but enemy resistance began to stiffen in the area of Carlentini and Lentini, in the path of the 50th Division.

The 51st (Highland) Division and two infantry brigades of the 1st Canadian Division, supported by units of the 23rd Armoured Brigade, landed on the left flank of 8th Army and proceeded inland. The 3rd Canadian brigade came in later with the 12th Army Tank Regiment (Three Rivers Regiment) of the 1st Canadian Army Tank Brigade.

The other two tank regiments and brigade headquarters landed at Syracuse after it was captured but they did not participate in any action during this campaign. In August, the brigade was redesignated 'armoured' and accordingly the same designation was assumed by its three regiments.

Meanwhile, during the night of 13 July, the 1st Parachute Brigade left North Africa in 105 Dakota and eleven Albemarle aircraft and eight Waco and eleven Horsa gliders. Their objective was the Primosole bridge, five miles south of Catania. Unfortunately, the Allied fleet mistook the identity of the formation and opened fire on the aircraft. More damage was later inflicted by the Axis anti-aircraft defences. Several aircraft crashed into the sea and on the beaches and in the ensuing confusion the paratroopers were dropped and the gliders were released in haste. As a result, only 250 men, out of 1,900, reached the Primosole bridge.

Coincidentally, the British airlanding was matched by a German airlanding in the same area of troops from the German 1st Parachute Division sent to defend the city of Catania. A fierce battle began around the Primosole bridge and in the area of Lentini where the 50th Division and the 4th Armoured Brigade pressed northwards in order to relieve the British paratroopers.

By the late afternoon, the latter regrouped on the south side of the bridge. During the night, they were compelled to retreat towards a hill which was already in British hands. Relief arrived on the following day at dusk, in the form of a Sherman tank followed by a battalion of the Durhams which, during the morning of 16 July captured the Primosole bridge from the

Germans. Although the bridge was taken and a bridgehead was established north of the Simeto river, the advance of 13th Corps nevertheless came to a standstill.

## Navy

The naval support was magnificent. This was the largest landing operation carried out until that time and required the most meticulous organisation. The first to land were the Combined Operations Reconnaissance and Pilotage Parties, from submarines. Later, the submarines acted as beacons to guide the landing craft to their beaches.

The warships had the tasks of defending the fleet from air, underwater and surface attacks, and of supporting the land forces, softening the enemy defences on land by preliminary bombardment and later by shelling targets in direct support of army units. This latter facet of naval activity, direct support, was invaluable, particularly at Gela on 11 July and later at Salerno and Anzio.

The last task of the navy was to supply the forces on land, which became an ever demanding assignment as the war progressed.

## US 7th Army

The American 7th Army had not had a clear objective after its landing apart from the role of supporting the 8th Army's strike towards Messina. It had, however, a much greater area in which to manoeuvre and to occupy than its British counterpart. The two armies were to meet at Ragusa which meant that Enna, Caltagirone and most of the island were in the American operational area.

### Airborne

The 505th Parachute Infantry Regiment and one battalion of the 504th, from the 82nd Airborne 'All American' Division, spearheaded the invasion encountering the same stormy weather conditions as the British. The paratroopers landed too far inland and were scattered over a vast area, and only about three companies captured their initial objectives. Nevertheless, the operation achieved the unforeseen effect of confusing and demoralising the defenders who assumed that they had been attacked in depth by a vast airborne army.

Maj. General Matthew B. Ridgway, the divisional commander, landed by boat on 10 July to assess the situation. He decided to reinforce his troops on the hills by launching the remainder of the 504th regiment during the following night. The C-47s loaded with troops arrived at the end of a German air raid and the fleet gunners mistook them for German aircraft and opened fire. Twenty-three aircraft were shot down and ninety-seven men were killed by error during that night.

### Land Army

The US 2nd Corps comprised the 1st and the 45th Divisions. The former had already fought in Tunisia, while the latter came from

Maj. General Anders greets Prince Umberto of Savoy on the Cassino front in May 1944. The Prince wears Italian uniform with rank insignia of Marshal of Italy. *Polish Institute and Sikorski Museum Collection*

the United States, via Oran where it had trained in amphibious operations. The 3rd Division was to land to the west of 2nd Corps, under direct control of 7th Army. The 2nd Armored Division and part of the 9th Infantry Division were in floating reserve. Gela was in the centre of the American landing sector.

The 1st Division commenced landing at 2.45 a.m. on Saturday, 10 July, flanked by the 3rd, towards Licata and by the 45th towards Scoglitti. The landing operations were preceded by naval bombardment and spearheaded by US Rangers.

On Sunday, the 'Hermann Göring' and the 'Livorno' counter-attacked from the high ground behind Gela and Licata, respectively. A fierce twenty-four hour battle developed, settled by the intervention of naval guns. The Axis forces retreated and, as soon as the beach was consolidated, the 2nd Armored Division started to disembark and the invasion forces began to spread inland.

General Bradley established his 2nd Corps HQ at Vittoria. The corps' main axis of advance was aimed towards Enna and Caltanissetta to the north while the 3rd and 82nd Divisions were ordered to advance westwards, towards Marsala and Trapani. These two divisions became part of a provisional corps.

### German reinforcements

Hitler was fully aware of the developments. On 13 July, as the situation deteriorated rapidly, he ordered two German divisions, the 1st 'Fallschirm' and the 29th 'Panzer-Grenadier', supported by a German corps HQ, to intervene immediately.

It had become apparent to the defenders that any hope of holding Sicily was futile. From the beginning there were not enough troops on the island, the coastal defences proved useless, the 54th 'Napoli' Division had been lost and, if the US 2nd Corps' advance could not be halted, the Italian 12th Corps was in danger of being trapped on the western side of the island.

The Allies' plan to capture Messina as soon as possible, by the shortest route, was evident. Therefore, the Axis' immediate solution was to stop the 8th Army's advance in order to give time to the Axis formations in the west to retreat and regroup in the north-eastern corner of Sicily. From there, they could be ferried across the Straits of Messina, as a last, but pre-organised, solution. Consequently, two German parachute regiments and their support units were airlifted from Rome to the Catania Plain and the 29th Division came across from Italy.

### American break-through

By 15 July, the American bridge-head extended inland to Niscemi, Canicatti and Palma di Montechiaro, with columns exploiting any possible route of advance. Caltanissetta fell on 18 July, while in the west, Agrigento and Porto Empedocle were captured, the latter by the Rangers. On 17 July, the 82nd Division began to advance and covered a distance of 150 miles in six days, capturing Trapani, Castellamare and Capo San Vito.

The 1st Canadian Division, on the left flank of the 8th Army, advanced through Grammichele and Caltagirone, captured Piazza Armerina with American help, and in a joint attack, Americans and Canadians captured Enna on 20 July.

Palermo fell to the US 2nd Corps on 22 July. At this stage, the corps' 45th Division turned right towards Messina. Its 1st Division and the Canadians also turned right but farther inland.

## British 8th Army

By this time, the 8th Army's line ran from the bridge-head at Primosole along the river Dittaino to Enna. It was evident that the Germans were forming a line of defence which ran from south of Mount Etna, through Troina and to the Tyrrhenian Sea. The 29th 'Panzer-Grenadier' and the 'Hermann Göring' defended Leonforte and Agira in the central sector.

Allied Forces HQ decided to continue the 8th Army's offensive from its left flank, behind Mount Etna and the 78th Infantry Division joined 30th Corps in Sicily. A Canadian brigade crossed the Dittaino on the night of 29/30 July and the 78th Division began its advance towards the fortress town of Centuripe, defended by the German 3rd Parachute Regiment and units of the 'Hermann Göring'. A fierce battle developed during the first two days of August. Suddenly, on the 3rd, the Germans retreated.

## The Invasion

The Americans captured Nicosia and the Canadians took Regalbuto and Agira on 3 August. On the same day, the Germans began to retreat from Catania, pursued by 13th Corps. Catania fell on 5 August. Troina fell to the US 1st Division on 6 August. S. Stefano, on the Tyrrhenian coast, had been taken earlier but in the meantime the French Goums were approaching S. Fratello, farther up the road, from the mountains. The British 78th Division occupied Aderno and Bronte and, to the north, met American troops coming along Highway 120, at Randazzo.

Mount Etna had been bypassed. Messina became the next objective of a race between American and British forces, while the Germans were evacuating through the Straits.

The British 13th Corps which, according to the initial plans should have captured Messina, proceeded slowly along the western road, hampered by German rearguard actions and demolitions. On 15 August, it reached Taormina while the US 2nd Corps on the north road had already arrived at Milazzo.

On 22 July, No 2 Commando arrived in Sicily from Gibraltar. On the evening of 15 August, together with units from the 4th Armoured Brigade, it was despatched to land at Scaletta Marina, about eight miles south of Messina, in a desperate attempt to speed up the advance. Brigadier Curry commanded the expedition.

Once disembarked, Curry realised that the 50th Division could not catch up with them because the road in between was blown in two places. Therefore, he decided to drive to Messina with the commandos and a squadron from the 'Sharpshooters'. Unknown

### Plate VII

A British regiment was composed of two, three or more battalions. Usually, the battalions were assigned to brigades of different divisions, but each retained its regimental title, preceded by the battalion's number, as shown in the orders of battle in the text.

As all the battalions of a regiment wore the same cap badge, to avoid repetition, only one regimental cap badge is shown following the order related to the divisions as they enter the battlefield.

This plate deals with the formation signs and the cap badges of the three British infantry divisions and one independent brigade which landed in Sicily. All the regimental badges of the battalions of the 5th Infantry Division are shown but, in the case of the 50th (Northumbrian) Infantry Division, its 69th Brigade included the 6th and 7th Battalions of the Green Howards and their cap badge is shown already within the 5th Division. The 151st Brigade was composed of three battalions of the Durham Light Infantry, and their cap badge is shown.

Two main patterns of formation signs were used, embroidered and printed, although the 'Y' of the 5th Division was also made of linen, sewn onto a khaki background.

The cap badges were made of metal. Shown here are the other ranks' pattern as the officers' pattern was similar but made of gilt and silver, or silver-plated, or wholly of bronze, for service dress.

5th INFANTRY DIVISION

The Cameronians
(Scottish Rifles)

The Royal
Inniskilling Fusiliers

The Wiltshire Regiment
(Duke of Edinburgh's)

The Green Howards
(Alexandra, Princess
of Wales' Own
Yorkshire Regiment)

The King's Own
Yorkshire Light
Infantry

The York and
Lancaster
Regiment

The Royal Scots
Fusiliers

The Northamptonshire
Regiment

Seaforth Highlanders
(Ross-shire Buffs,
The Duke of Albany's)

The Cheshire Regiment

50th (NORTHUMBRIAN)
INFANTRY DIVISION

The East Yorkshire Regiment
(The Duke of York's Own)

The Durham Light Infantry

51st (HIGHLAND)
INFANTRY DIVISION

The Queen's Own
Cameron Highlanders

The Black Watch
(Royal Highland Regiment)

The Argyll and
Sutherland Highlanders
(Princess Louise's)

The Gordon
Highlanders

The Middlesex Regiment
(The Duke of Cambridge's Own)

The Northumberland
Hussars

231st INFANTRY BRIGADE

The Devonshire
Regiment

The Dorsetshire
Regiment

to them, the Americans on the northern road executed a similar leap-frogging advance. When Curry and his men entered Messina, they met American patrols who were already there. Later, General Patton was received in front of the town hall.

The 7th Infantry Regiment of the US 3rd Division reached Messina on the evening of 16 August. The British units from Scaletta Marina entered the city by 1000 hours the following morning.

The Sicilian campaign lasted thirty-eight days.

---

**The Fortunes of War**

'My grandfather emigrated to America early this century but in 1939 my father decided to come back to Sicily where he bought this house.

'I was about 13 years old when the Germans arrived in Taormina. Field Marshal Kesselring set up his headquarters in the Monastery of San Domenico, which is now an hotel, and a signal station in our house, as it is on the cliffs overlooking the coast of Calabria.

'We moved temporarily to a nearby village, an old lady who remained in Taormina was put in charge of our possessions and she reported to us periodically. One day she turned up with the house keys and told us that the Germans had left, that they had given her the keys and that everything in the house was exactly as when we had left.

'Immediately we set out for Taormina but in the meantime the "Inglesi" had taken over our house and we found that, once again, it had become a signal station. We went back to the village!

'A few weeks later the old lady returned the keys again. The "Inglesi" had gone. Everything in the house was smashed. We had a grand piano which had disappeared.

'Not long after our return to the house an American officer arrived and asked my father if the US Army could use the premises as a rest house for officers. We did not need to move and in fact they would feed us and pay a rent.

'An offer that my father could not refuse. They did not give any trouble; they were asleep most of the time, day or night, they walked up to the centre and came back to sleep.

With the money from the Americans my father was able to turn the house into an hotel after the war.'
Hotel Owner, Taormina

---

# 2 THE INVASION OF SOUTHERN ITALY

Donald R. Paine in Rome just a few days after its capture in June 1944. He served in the 2nd Battalion, the Sherwood Foresters, 3rd Brigade, 1st Infantry Division, at Anzio, through Italy and on the 'Gothic' Line until February 1945. *D. R. Paine Collection*

## THE ITALIANS

By the middle of July 1943, Italy had lost its colonies and foreign troops were fighting on her soil. Contrary to Mussolini's expectations, every campaign had been a disaster – Greece, Russia, Africa – and every battle had been lost. It was clear that Sicily was undefendable and that the Italian peninsula was to become the next battlefield.

A dozen Italian divisions were stationed in Greece and on the Aegean islands. About twenty divisions were engaged in Albania and Yugoslavia against Communist partisans' warfare. Three were in the south of France. Seven divisions were stationed in the north of Italy, most of which were veterans from the Russian front where they had suffered appalling losses. Eleven divisions were in central Italy, four were on the islands of Sardinia and Corsica and only three infantry divisions were in the south of the peninsula. Except for six Alpine divisions, the 184th Parachute Division 'Nembo' and two armoured divisions stationed in central Italy, the rest were infantry divisions, the vast majority 'on foot'. By this time Italy had difficulties in supplying this vast army; undoubtedly, the war was lost.

During the night of 24–25 July 1943 the Fascist Grand Council met in Rome to consider the situation. At this meeting, Mussolini lost the vote of confidence from the other members of the council, which led to the collapse of the Fascist Government in Italy. Mussolini was arrested after a visit to the king the following day, and the king instructed Marshal Pietro Badoglio to form a new government.

Badoglio declared his government's allegiance to the Axis but at the same time feelers were put out by the new government to the Allies through diplomatic channels asking about the possibility of an armistice. An Italian envoy called upon the British ambassador in Madrid on 15 August. Another meeting took place four days later in Lisbon. The Allies could only offer unconditional surrender. They could not disclose to the Italians their plans for their imminent landings on mainland Italy.

On 31 August, another meeting took place at Syracuse between the Italian envoy and General Eisenhower's representatives. The Italian Government accepted the terms of surrender. However, the envoy declared that his government was powerless until the Allies had actually invaded Italy because, in the meantime the Germans were pouring troops into Italy and the Italian Government could not refuse its Axis allies help until the declaration of the armistice.

78th INFANTRY DIVISION

The Lancashire
Fusiliers

The East Surrey
Regiment

The Queen's Own
Royal West
Kent Regiment

The Buffs
(Royal East
Kent Regiment)

38th (IRISH) IMFANTRY BRIGADE

The Royal Irish Fusiliers
(Princess Victoria's)

The London
Irish Rifles

Princess Louise's
Kensington Regiment

4th ARMOURED
BRIGADE

23rd ARMOURED
BRIGADE

Glamorgan Yeomanry

The Queen's
Own Royal
Glasgow Yeomanry

168th INFANTRY BRIGADE

3rd County of
London Yeomanry
(Sharpshooters)

The London Scottish
The Gordon Highlanders

The Royal Berkshire
Regiment (Princess
Charlotte of Wales's)

43rd INFANTRY BRIGADE

The Somerset
Light Infantry
(Prince Albert's)

The Royal Norfolk
Regiment

The King's
Royal Rifle Corps

Royal Tank Regiment

The Shropshire Yeomanry

The City of London
Yeomanry
(Rough Riders)

**Plate VIII**

The 78th Infantry Division fought with distinction at the battle of Centuripe which broke the German line of defence behind Mount Etna. The shamrock surmounted by one green stripe was worn by the 38th (Irish) Infantry Brigade on the sleeves below the formation sign. The Kensingtons, the divisional machine-gun battalion, wore a regimental flash of red and grey.

Lt Colonel H. E. L. Bredin, DSO, MC, commanded the 2nd London Irish Rifles from July 1944 onwards. He wore the Irish caubeen with the hackle and the shamrock – the leaves of the latter seem rather more square than those of the badge illustrated on the left.

The Glamorgan and the Glasgow Yeomanry were artillery units but still retained their yeomanry cap badges.

The badges of the 4th and 23rd Armoured Brigade are displayed on the left hand side of this plate. On the other side are the cap badges of the 168th Infantry Brigade, of the 56th Division, which was attached to the 50th for the duration of the campaign of Sicily. The officers' cap badge of the Royal Berkshire Regiment depicts the dragon below the crown set on three coils of rope, in bronze.

The 43rd Infantry Brigade was in Sicily from November 1943 to June 1944 and therefore saw no action.

Lastly, the Shropshire Yeomanry and the Rough Riders, converted to artillery role, were at that time in reserve, under command of Allied Forces HQ.

The armistice between Italy and the United Nations was signed on 3 September and came into effect at 5.30 p.m. on 8 September 1943, the eve of Operation AVALANCHE, the Allied landing at Salerno. The possibility of airlanding the US 82nd Airborne Division on Rome's airfields was considered but cancelled at the last moment. General Maxwell Taylor and Colonel William T. Gardiner went secretly to Rome to reconnoitre before the operation, codenamed GIANT II. On the evening of 7 September they visited General Giacomo Carboni, commander of the Italian troops in that area, who informed them that the airfields were in German hands. Later, Marshal Badoglio told them that nineteen German divisions were already in Italy and asked Maxwell Taylor to postpone the declaration of the armistice. This could not be done but GIANT II was cancelled.

## THE ALLIES AND THE GERMANS

It was necessary to keep Germany occupied on a second front to prevent it pounding the Soviet Union with all its forces. However the plans for the invasions of Sicily and Italy were not part of a co-ordinated strategy to attack the Axis powers from the south. The British favoured this strategy. The Americans, however, were keen to confront Germany directly, through northern France, but the Allies were not ready for this major, final campaign.

### The Allied Planning

Italy's wish to reach an armistice gave the Allies the feeling of a victory which could be followed by potentially great results. The 'Trident' Conference in Washington in May 1943 and the 'Quadrant' Conference in Quebec three months later envisaged a policy of exploiting the situation in order to eliminate Italy from the conflict and to keep the German forces fully engaged in the Mediterranean sector.

Before the end of the war in Sicily, plans were already under consideration for the invasion of Italy. Operation BAYTOWN, the landing near Reggio Calabria, was the logical continuation of the campaign in Sicily. The Straits of Messina being narrow, the crossing did not present serious difficulties. Furthermore, the Calabrian coastline did not seem to be particularly well defended.

Operation AVALANCHE was the codename for the landing at Salerno. Although one of the two corps concerned was British, it was an American venture.

The Italian surrender led to a great deal of confusion in planning. Operation GIANT II was approved and then cancelled. Operation SLAPSTICK, the landing at Taranto, was decided at the last moment because, according to information obtained from the Italians, there were no German troops in that area.

Several formations could not be used in Italy because they were due to be prepared for Operation OVERLORD, in Britain. The British 8th Army lost two infantry divisions, the 50th and 51st, immediately. The 231st Infantry Brigade, the 1st Airborne

Division except one brigade, and the 7th Armoured Division returned to Britain later. The US 7th Army lost two infantry divisions, the 1st and 9th, and the 2nd Armored Division, and then, after AVALANCHE, the 82nd Airborne Division.

## The German Defence

During the eighteen days between the fall of Sicily and the British landing in mainland Calabria, the Germans withdrew the bulk of their armour from the Calabrian mountains and started to organise a plan of defence in readiness for future events. Another six days elapsed before the landings at Taranto and Salerno. By then, the Germans had a clear picture of the Allies' intentions. The Italians had no part in the German defensive plans as it was evident that they were completely unprepared for any eventuality.

The available German troops were organised into two armoured corps, the 14th and 76th Panzer Corps, under the supervision of the 10th Army, commanded by General Heinrich von Vietinghoff. The 76th Corps defended the regions of Calabria and Puglie while the other corps was in the region of Campania waiting for further developments.

Another thirteen divisions and smaller army formations plus a corps of the *Luftwaffe* were stationed in central and northern Italy, ready to intervene.

**10th Army**

| 14th Panzer Corps | 76th Panzer Corps |
|---|---|
| 16th Panzer Division | 26th Panzer Division |
| Panzer Division 'Hermann Göring' | 29th Panzer Grenadier Division |
| 15th Panzer Grenadier Division | 1st Parachute Division |

# THE SOUTHERN LANDINGS

## Operation BAYTOWN

Operation BAYTOWN had to take place as soon as possible in order to free the Straits of Messina for Allied ships in time for AVALANCHE, and to attract the German divisions to the south thereby allowing the US 5th Army to trap them at their rear from Salerno. The Germans, however, waited for the next move.

The British 13th Corps was selected for the operation.

**13th Corps**

| 3 September 1943 | No 3 Commando |
|---|---|
| 1st Canadian Infantry Division | No 40 (Royal Marine) Commando |
| 5th Infantry Division | Special Raiding Squadron |
| 231st Infantry Brigade | |

The operation began in the early morning of 3 September 1943, preceded by an artillery bombardment. A small party of men from No 3 Commando were put ashore near Bova Marina a few days before the invasion. The remaining troops and No 40 (Royal Marine) Commando spearheaded the main landing force during the night of 2/3 September. The first unit to land, however, was the Special Raiding Squadron, going ashore at Bagnara which was held until the 15th Infantry Brigade reached them on 4 September.

Little opposition was met. The 13th Corps advanced harassed only by demolitions and rearguard units, a few Germans, and Italian paratroopers from the 185th Regiment 'Nembo'. The latter were highly motivated troops many of whom opted to continue the war with the Germans after the armistice.

---

**Assaulting 'Fortress Europe'**

'Yes, of course, I have seen the "Inglesi" landing. I was young then but I will never forget!

'We were living in a village on the coast, up that way, and after we lost Sicily they started to shell Calabria and we knew that sooner or later they would come across. Our village was never bombarded, but Reggio was badly hit and farther north, where we are now.

'Then suddenly the gunfire increased and one night we knew, I don't know why, that they would land. We kept an eye on the sea and then a shout: – "*Arrivano gli Inglesi!*" (The English are coming).

'I was on the beach, it was still dark, I remember vividly, and all the village population was there. Dozens, perhaps hundreds of boats were crossing the straits. Small black dots on the horizon, and becoming bigger as they approached. It seemed that they were all going to land just in front of us and at that stage we were too frightened to run away.

'There were no Italian or German soldiers there as they had gone days before, there was only us from the village there, on the beach!

'The "Inglesi" landed and began running towards the woods behind us, they just ignored us. More landed and disappeared into the hills.

'That's all!'

Villa S. Giovanni, restaurant owner.

---

**Operation SLAPSTICK**

As BAYTOWN was executed, hurried preparations were made for shipping the 1st Airborne Division to Taranto. On 1 September, the division was put on a week's notice to embark at Bizerta. Popski's Private Army was to provide five jeeps and their crews to land with the first wave of troops.

A new British corps entered the Italian battlefield, the 5th Corps.

**5th Corps**

22 September 1943
  1st Airborne Division
  8th Indian Division
  78th Infantry Division

4th Armoured Brigade
2nd Special Air Service
No 1 Demolition Squadron
  (Popski's Private Army)

## 8th Indian Division

The division was formed in October 1940 and was sent to Persia in 1941 and later to Iraq. It joined the 8th Army in 1942. Entering at the time of the retreat to Alamein, it participated in the campaign in the Western Desert, and in the subsequent operations.

**8th Indian Division**

September 1943
17th Indian Infantry Brigade
  1st The Royal Fusiliers (City of
    London Regiment)
  1/12th Frontier Force Regiment
  1/5th Royal Gurkha Rifles
    (Frontier Force)
19th Indian Infantry Brigade
  1/5th The Essex Regiment
  2/8th Punjab Regiment
  6/13th Frontier Force Rifles
21st Indian Infantry Brigade
  5th Royal West Kent Regiment
  1/5th Maratta Light Infantry
  3/15th Punjab Regiment

Divisional Troops
Royal Artillery
  3rd, 52nd and 53rd Field
    Regiments
  4th Maratta Anti-tank Regiment
  26th Light Anti-aircraft Regiment
Royal Engineers
  7th, 66th and 69th Field
    Companies
  47th Field Park Company
  (All Bengal Sappers and Miners)
Royal Signals
  8th Indian Division
Reconnaissance Corps
  6th Duke of Connaught's Own
    (Bengal) Lancers
Machine-gun Battalion
  5/5th Maratta Light Infantry

## No 1 Demolition Squadron: Popski's Private Army

Popski was the nickname of this unit's commander, Major Vladimir Peniakoff, a Belgian of Russian extraction who lived in Egypt. In the early 1930s, Peniakoff had learned, as a hobby, to travel the desert with the aid of a sun compass. In October 1940, he volunteered to serve in the British Army. He served in the

### Plate IX

The US 7th Army landed in Sicily spearheaded by the 82nd Airborne 'All American' Division and by three battalions of Rangers.

The badge of the latter, illustrated, was later worn exclusively by the 2nd and 5th Battalions in France and Germany, the scroll type badge being used by the Rangers in Italy (see Plate XI).

During the Italian campaign, the US Army did not use a great variety of badges as the wearing of metal and enamel units' distinctive insignia had been discontinued earlier in 1943 for the duration of the war. The shoulder sleeve insignia, commonly known as shoulder patches, identified divisions and higher formations, and were machine woven in the USA.

The 'hat patch' was worn on the left side of the garrison cap by airborne troops: paratroopers had a parachute, glider-borne troops a glider, both on blue or red background for infantry or artillery, respectively. Paraglider units wore a glider superimposed on a parachute, with light blue outer edge for infantry, red for artillery. The latter badge was not worn in Italy but it is illustrated because it shows both the parachute and the glider displayed separately in the other two badges. New badges with the glider facing the opposite direction were adopted in 1943 for officers who were instructed to wear the patch on the right side of the cap.

Maj. General Matthew B. Ridgway, wearing parachutist's combat dress is depicted below with another officer of the 82nd Airborne Division. The latter had his rank insignia on the jacket which he has taken off.

Two infantrymen wearing different types of field uniform complete this plate of illustrations.

Battery commanders and staff of the 171st Field Artillery Battalion, 45th Infantry Division, in a locality north of the Tiber river. *45th Infantry Division Museum*

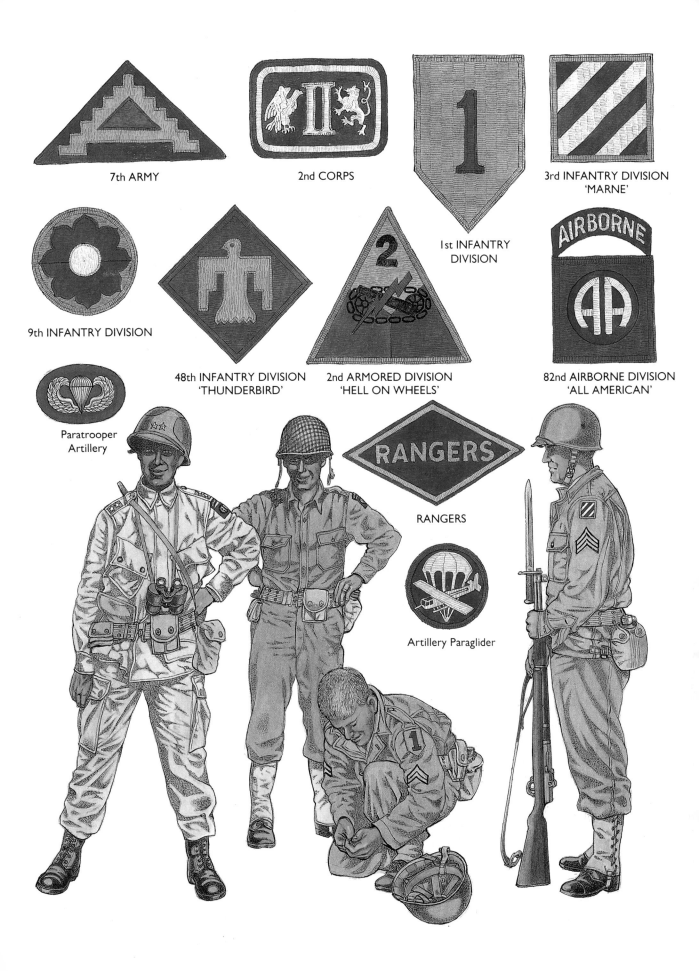

7th ARMY

2nd CORPS

3rd INFANTRY DIVISION 'MARNE'

1st INFANTRY DIVISION

9th INFANTRY DIVISION

48th INFANTRY DIVISION 'THUNDERBIRD'

2nd ARMORED DIVISION 'HELL ON WHEELS'

82nd AIRBORNE DIVISION 'ALL AMERICAN'

Paratrooper Artillery

RANGERS

Artillery Paraglider

Libyan Arab Force within which he formed a commando for the purpose of gathering information behind the enemy lines. He also operated with the Long Range Desert Group.

Popski's Private Army (P.P.A.) was formed in October 1942 under the provisional name of No 1 Demolition Squadron, with an establishment of twenty-three all ranks. Its designated tasks were reconnaissance and gathering information behind enemy lines. It operated in Libya after the break-through at Alamein and was the first 8th Army unit to make contact with the 1st Army in Tunisia.

### The Taranto Landing

The convoy that ferried the 1st Airborne Division and P.P.A. left Tunisia on 7 September 1943. Next day, the troops heard the announcement of the armistice with Italy and were given their destination, Taranto. No opposition was encountered on landing but unfortunately HMS *Abdiel* struck a mine in the harbour and fifty-eight men of the 6th (Royal Welch) Parachute Battalion were killed and 154 were injured.

The 78th Infantry Division went from Sicily to Italy in the period from 19 to 29 September. The men were shipped directly to Taranto. Most of the vehicles and guns, ferried across the Straits of Messina, went by road to Crotone and then by sea to Taranto.

The 4th Armoured Brigade received orders to move on 16 September. All tracked vehicles were ferried directly to the bridgehead at Taranto by sea; wheeled vehicles went across the Straits by ferry, thence by road to Taranto.

The occupation of the Puglie region proceeded rapidly, delayed only by demolitions and rearguard actions performed by German parachute units. The bulk of the German forces waited for the Allies on the high ground above Salerno. Foggia was captured on 27 September and the advance continued towards Termoli.

### Operation AVALANCHE

The US 5th Army was entrusted to Lt General Mark W. Clark, on his first operational command, and was formed in North Africa from British and American contingents.

Sergeant Doug Morgan, Royal Canadian Ordnance Corps. He wears a cloth shoulder title, the rectangular formation sign and his trade badge above the sergeant's chevrons.
*R. Goode Collection*

| US 5th Army | British 10th Corps |
|---|---|
| US 6th Corps | 46th (North Midland) Infantry |
| 3rd Infantry Division 'Marne' | Division |
| 34th Infantry Division 'Red Bull' | 56th (London) Division |
| 36th Infantry Division 'Texas' | 7th Armoured Division |
| 45th Infantry Division | 23rd Armoured Brigade |
| 'Thunderbird' | |

The following units were under the command of 10th Corps as they landed on the left side of the corps:

| 1st, 3rd and 4th Battalion Rangers | No 41 (Royal Marine) Commando |
|---|---|
| No 2 Commando | |

### 34th Infantry Division 'Red Bull'

The 34th Division was inducted for service once again on 10 February 1941, composed of National Guard units from North and South Dakota, Iowa and Minnesota. The division trained at Camp Claiborne, Louisiana. Between January and May 1942, the division was transferred to Northern Ireland. It was the first American division to be sent to the European Theatre of Operations.

After amphibious training in Scotland, the division departed for North Africa where it landed near Algiers, ahead of the 78th British division. The Americans were in charge of the initial operations and of approaching the French garrisons because the French were more amiable towards the Americans than towards the British at that crucial time. Subsequently, many units were used independently until March 1943 when the whole division fought at Fondouk Gap and in May on Hill 609.

Later, the 34th Division was held in reserve for future operations and joined the 5th Army, in training at the Invasion Training Centre for the landing at Salerno.

**34th Infantry Division 'Red Bull'**

| | |
|---|---|
| 133rd, 135th and 168th Infantry Regiments | 109th Medical Battalion |
| 125th, 151st, 175th and 185th Field Artillery Battalions | 34th Signal Company |
| | 734th Ordnance Company |
| 109th Engineers Battalion | 34th Quartermaster Company |
| | 34th Reconnaissance Troop |

Lieutenant John O. Gaultney, US 91st Division, near Casole D'Elsa on 5 July 1944. He still wears the M.1938 canvas leggings, later replaced by boots with integral anklets. *B. Livengood Collection*

### 36th Infantry Division 'Texas'

During World War One, the 36th Division was formed from units from Texas and Oklahoma. During the post-war reorganisation of the National Guard, the Oklahoma contingent went to the 45th Division, and the 36th thus became a wholly Texas formation.

In November 1940, the division was organised at Camp Bowie. Later, it trained at Camp Blanding, Florida, and at Camp Edwards, Massachusetts, taking part in the 1941 Louisiana Manoeuvres.

The 'Texas' Division arrived in North Africa on 13 April 1943. After a new period of training, it was assigned to 6th Corps in readiness for Operation AVALANCHE.

**36th Infantry Division 'Texas'**

| | |
|---|---|
| 141st, 142nd and 143rd Infantry Regiments | 111th Medical Battalion |
| 131st, 132nd, 133rd and 155th Field Artillery Battalions | 36th Signal Company |
| | 736th Ordnance Company |
| 111th Engineers Battalion | 36th Quartermaster Company |
| | 36th Reconnaissance Troop |

### 46th (North Midland) Infantry Division

The 46th was a second-line territorial division formed initially by the 137th, 138th and 139th Brigades. Thus composed, it went to France in April 1940 for training and labour duties, leaving behind most of its divisional support units. In France, it became part of

5th CORPS

8th INDIAN DIVISION

The Royal Fusiliers
(City of London
Regiment)

12th Frontier
Force Regiment

5th Royal
Gurkha Rifles

The Essex
Regiment

8th Punjab
Regiment

13th Royal Frontier
Force Regiment

5th Maharatta
Light Infantry

15th Punjab
Regiment

6th Duke of
Connaught's Own
(Bengal) Lancers

No1 Demolition
Squadron
(Popski's Private Army)

2nd Army Group
Royal Artillery

Indian Artillery

6th Army Group
Royal Artillery

No2 Commando

Indian Engineers

Indian Signal
Corps

Royal Indian
Army Service Corps

Indian Army
Ordnance Corps

Indian Electrical and
Mechanical Engineers

Indian Military
Police

Indian Army
Medical Corps

**Plate X**

The 8th was the first of three Indian divisions to enter the Italian campaign.

Sikhs, Punjabis, Maharattas and some other sects were allowed to wear their traditional types of head-dress, together with standard British Army uniforms and equipment, as shown by the two soldiers illustrated. The sapper on the right is operating a Polish mine detector.

Each infantry brigade of an Indian infantry division contained one British and two Indian battalions and the artillery contingent was usually British, but the rest of the division was composed of Indian units. The supporting corps of the Indian Army had their own cap badges, which have been illustrated.

No 1 Demolition Squadron (Popski's Private Army) landed at Taranto. The cap badges for this unit, based on the design of an astrolabe, were initially made in Egypt in brass and in silver, later, towards the end of the war, some were made by a silversmith in Rome. The shoulder title of this unit depicted the initials 'P.P.A.' in red on dark blue, changed later to white letters on black.

No 2 Commando landed in the bay of Salerno on 9 September 1943. By then, the only official insignia allowed for wearing was the curved shoulder title. Nonetheless, it is possible that the 'S/S' – Special Service – cap badge worn in 1941–42 was still in use.

the lines of communication of the British Expeditionary Force. After the German offensive, one brigade was evacuated from Dunkirk while the rest of the division left France from Normandy and Brittany.

In 1942, the 137th Brigade, which converted to armour, was replaced by the 128th Infantry Brigade formed by Hampshire battalions. After a period of organisation and training, the 46th Division was transferred to North Africa as part of the 1st Army. After the battle of El Kouriza, the division participated in the advance towards Tunis, with 5th Corps. At the end of July the 46th Division was transferred to 10th Corps, in training for the landing at Salerno.

### 46th (North Midland) Infantry Division

128th Infantry Brigade
  1/4th, 5th and 2nd The Hampshire Regiments
138th Infantry Brigade
  6th The Lincolnshire Regiment
  2/4th The King's Own Yorkshire Light Infantry
  6th The Yorks and Lancashire Regiment
139th Infantry Brigade
  2/5th The Leicestershire Regiment
  5th The Sherwood Foresters (Nottinghamshire and Derbyshire Regiment)
  16th The Durham Light Infantry

Divisional Troops
Royal Artillery
  70th, 71st and 172nd Field Regiments
  58th Anti-tank Regiment
  115th Light Anti-aircraft Regiment
Royal Engineers
  270th, 271st and 272nd Field Companies
  273rd Field Park Company
Royal Signals
  46th Division
Reconnaissance Corps
  46th Regiment
Machine-gun Battalion
  2/7th The Middlesex Regiment (The Duke of Cambridge's Own)

### 56th (London) Division

Originally known as the 1st London Division and formed by the 1st and 2nd London Infantry Brigades, this division was a first line Territorial Army formation, organised as a motor division. In June 1940, it became an infantry division and was redesignated 56th (London) Division in November 1940. In July 1940, the 35th Infantry Brigade joined the other two. In November, the three brigades were redesignated the 167th, 168th and 169th (London) Infantry Brigades, respectively.

The division left Britain for Iraq at the end of August 1942, arriving there on 4 November. It then moved to Palestine and then Egypt, before proceeding to North Africa to join 10th Corps in Tunisia. It participated in the battle of Enfidaville and in the capture of Tunis.

After the end of the hostilities in Africa, the 56th Division temporarily lost its 168th Brigade and some divisional troops, which were put under 13th Corps' command and later under the 50th (Northumberland) Infantry Division which was short of one brigade for the landings in Sicily. On 13 July 1943, the 168th Brigade landed in Sicily and remained on the island until 10 October when it embarked for Salerno.

51

The rest of the division, with the other two brigades and the 201st Guards Motor Brigade as reinforcement, landed at Salerno on 9 September 1943.

**56th (London) Division**

167th (London) Infantry Brigade
  8th (1st City of London Battalion)
    The London Regiment (City of London Regiment)
  9th (2nd City of London Battalion)
    The London Regiment (City of London Regiment)
  7th The Oxfordshire and Buckinghamshire Light Infantry
169th (London) Infantry Brigade
  2/5th The Queen's Royal Regiment (West Surrey)
  2/6th (Bermondsey) The Queen's Royal Regiment (West Surrey)
  2/7th (Southwark) The Queen's Royal Regiment (West Surrey)
201st Guards Motor Brigade*
  3rd Coldstream Guards
  6th Grenadier Guards

Divisional Troops
Royal Artillery
  64th, 65th and 113th Field Regiments
  67th Anti-tank Regiment
  100th Light Anti-aircraft Regiment
Royal Engineers
  42nd, 220th, 221st and 501st Field Companies
  563rd Field Park Company
Royal Signals
  56th Division
Reconnaissance Corps
  44th Regiment
Machine-gun Battalion
  6th The Cheshire Regiment

*This brigade comprised RASC, RAMC, etc, units as a brigade group.

### 7th Armoured Division

In the autumn of 1938 an armoured formation was raised in Egypt under the title of Matruh Mobile Force. After several redesignations and reorganisations, this formation became the famous 7th Armoured Division – the 'Desert Rats' of the Western Desert. To its nickname, it owes its unusual formation sign. The division took part in every major battle in the Western Desert, Egypt, Libya and Tunisia, from Sidi Barrani in December 1940 to Tunis in May 1943.

The 4th and the 7th were its original armoured brigades. The latter was withdrawn from the desert after the battle of Sidi Rezegh at the end of November 1941 and was sent to Burma in

A friendship is struck! A Polish private on the left shaking hands with an Italian sergeant who, however, wears the 'Poland' title. The Italian was obviously attached to the Polish Corps, perhaps as an interpreter. The markings on the lorry identify the 5th 'Kresowa' Division, 18th 'Lwowski' Rifle Battalion. *Polish Institute and Sikorski Museum Collection*

February 1942. At the same time, the 4th Armoured Brigade became an armoured brigade group and fought the rest of the campaign under the operational command of different formations, although mainly under the 1st and 7th Armoured Divisions.

In September 1942, the 22nd Armoured Brigade was attached from the 1st to the 7th Armoured Division. In November, the 131st Lorried Infantry Brigade became the divisional infantry contingent of the 7th Armoured Division.

The division disembarked at Salerno on 15 September 1943.

### 7th Armoured Division

22nd Armoured Brigade
    4th County of London Yeomanry
      (Sharpshooters)
    1st Royal Tank Regiment
    5th Royal Tank Regiment
    1st The Rifle Brigade (Prince
      Consort's Own)
131st Lorried Infantry Brigade
    1/5th The Queen's Royal Regiment
      (West Surrey)
    1/6th (Bermondsey) The Queen's
      Royal Regiment (West Surrey)
    1/7th (Southwark) The Queen's
      Royal Regiment (West Surrey)
    'C' Company, 1st The Cheshire
      Regiment (MG)

Divisional Troops
Royal Armoured Corps
    11th Hussars (Prince Albert's Own)
Royal Artillery
    3rd and 5th Royal Horse Artillery
    146th (Pembroke and Cardigan) Field
      Regiment
    65th (Norfolk Yeomanry) Anti-tank
      Regiment
    15th Light Anti-aircraft Regiment
Royal Engineers
    4th and 621st Field Squadrons
    143rd Field Park Squadron
Royal Signals
    7th Armoured Division

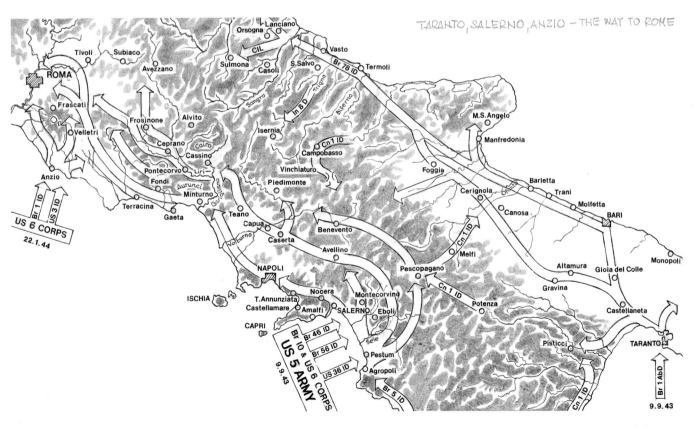

## The Salerno Landing

The landing in the bay of Salerno took place a few hours after the announcement of the armistice with Italy early on the morning of 9 September. The main objective of the operation was the capture of the port of Naples. In order to accomplish this task, the 46th Division, landing in the north, was to capture Salerno and move towards Nocera, supported by the 7th Armoured Division. Commandos and Rangers, supported by tanks and artillery, were to land farther north with the task of aiding 46th Division on its left flank. The 56th Division and the US 6th Corps were to take the towns of Battipaglia and Eboli and to cut communications with southern Italy.

The landings went according to plan, and were opposed by sporadic defence on the beaches. The 46th and 56th divisions of 10th Corps and the 36th Division of 6th Corps landed in the first wave. There was a gap of about six miles between the two corps. The US 45th Division commenced to land on 10 September.

**Plate XI**

The US 5th Army landed at Salerno under the command of Lt General Mark W. Clark (see Plate XXVIII/A). After a fierce battle around the beachhead, they conquered Naples.

This army was formed by an American and a British corps which supervised divisions of their own nationality. One formation, the 1st Special Service Force, comprised US and Canadian citizens, organised by the US Army and wearing American uniforms. Their shoulder insignia depicted an Indian spear head. Their branch insignia was that of the Special Forces, the crossed arrows. Their cap braid was red, white and blue.

The US 34th Division's insignia showed a bull's skull on the backing shape of an *olla*, a Mexican water flask. The 36th's badge was in the shape of a flint arrow head.

Some of these formations suffered severe casualties in the next campaigns, the 36th on crossing the river Rapido and the 34th during the first offensive at Cassino. Two Ranger battalions were virtually exterminated at Anzio.

The badge of the British 46th Division displayed an oak tree, suggestive of the north Midlands, and the 56th (London) Division's emblem was Dick Whittington's cat, on a red background.

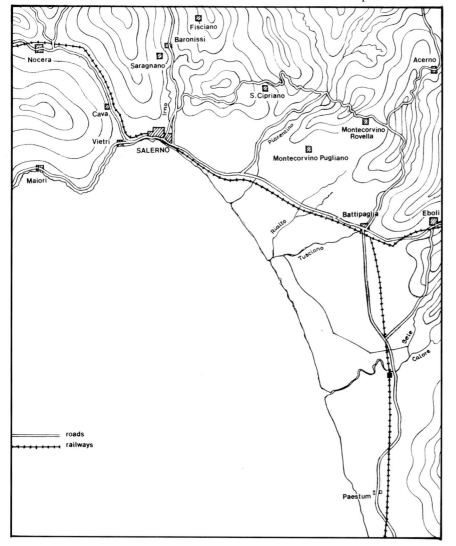

roads
railways

6th CORPS

5th ARMY

10th CORPS

34th INFANTRY DIVISION 'RED BULL'

36th INFANTRY DIVISION 'TEXAS'

The Lincolnshire Regiment

46th 'NORTH MIDLAND' INFANTRY DIVISION

The Manchester Regiment

The Royal Scots (The Royal Regiment)

The Leicestershire Regiment

The Sherwood Foresters (Nottinghamshire and Derbyshire Regiment)

1st, 3rd and 4th Ranger Battalion

1st SPECIAL SERVICE FORCE

56th 'LONDON' DIVISION

The Queen's Royal Regiment (West Surrey)

1st ARMORED DIVISION

No9 Commando

No43 (Royal Marine) Commando

The Oxfordshire and Buckinghamshire Light Infantry

The Royal Scots Greys (2nd Dragoons)

201st GUARDS MOTOR BRIGADE

Grenadier Guards

Coldstream Guards

As battalions were fanning out from the beach-head, they encountered increasing German opposition. Some battalions were unluckier than others. The 5th Hampshires met a German column supported by three tanks and were almost annihilated. The 167th Brigade captured Battipaglia, while on its left flank, the 169th reached Montecorvino airfield, destroying thirty-nine enemy aircraft still on the ground. The force that landed north-west of Salerno, the 46th Division, occupied Vietri on 10 September on their way to Nocera. On the southern perimeter, the 36th Division took Altavilla.

In danger of losing the high ground that dominated the battlefield, the Germans decided to counter-attack and recaptured Montecorvino and Battipaglia. Their major offensive started in the afternoon of 13 September, concentrating in between the river Sele and its affluent, the Calore, where there was a gap between the 45th and 36th Divisions of 6th Corps. A fierce battle began. The line in front of 10th Corps held but a battle group from 29th Panzer Grenadier Division smashed through in between the rivers only to find at their confluence that there was no bridge by which to proceed.

The Germans resumed the offensive on 14 September. The 16th and 29th Divisions advanced along the river Sele, aiming at the gap between the two corps, and the 26th Panzer Division attacked the British 56th, which was entrenched south-east of Battipaglia, but little was achieved. They attacked again on 16 September and the Panzer Corps clashed with the 46th (North Midland) Division but they did not have enough strength left to penetrate the Allies' positions.

Allied naval forces also ran into serious problems. On the morning of 11 September, the cruiser USS *Philadelphia* was hit by a new type of German weapon, a radio-controlled bomb which was launched and guided from aircraft. Subsequently, the USS *Savannah* and HMS *Uganda* were hit by these bombs and, although none were sunk, the three ships were severely damaged. The hospital ships *Newfoundland* and *Leinster* were also bombed, and the former was sunk. HMS *Warspite* was hit by a radio-controlled bomb on 16 September and withdrew to Malta.

All available ships were rallied to the bay of Salerno to bombard the German positions. Five escort carriers of the Royal Navy provided immediate air support, their aircraft flying 713 sorties in three days.

When the situation ashore reached its worst, on 14 September, suggestions were made to prepare plans for the 5th Army's re-embarkment, but the opposite view prevailed – land more troops and fight it out.

On 14 September, the 504th Parachute Infantry from the 82nd Airborne Division was dropped on the beach-head near Paestum. During the following night, the 505th was also dropped to reinforce the other regiment and the 509th Parachute Infantry Battalion was dropped near Avellino, to disrupt the German lines of communications. The rest of the 82nd Division landed by sea

A captain of the Polish Military Police wearing the third and latest pattern of collar insignia, with the grenade, made of metal and enamel. He has 'Poland' shoulder titles on both upper sleeves, the Mermaid shield on the left sleeve and the honorary sign of the 8th Army on the right. *Polish Institute and Sikorski Museum Collection*

or air and became part of the British 10th Corps. The British 7th Armoured Division began landing on 15 September while the 8th Army was approaching from the south, and made contact with the 5th Army at Agropoli on 17 September.

The Allied air forces never gave a moment of respite to the German defenders. On each of the crucial days, over 1,000 sorties were flown to support the troops on the beach-head. By September, the North-West African Air Force had moved to Sicily: eleven Spitfire, two Boston and one (No 600 Squadron) Beaufighter squadrons, not to mention the forces of the US Army Air Forces, or the fact that day by day new airfields were becoming available in mainland Italy. The Allies had won total air supremacy.

While Allied aircraft hit them from the air, the heavy guns of the Allied ships pounded the German positions incessantly, and with accuracy, even breaking up local tank assaults. Confronted with defeat, the Germans began to withdraw on 17 September, starting from their most southerly positions while 14th Panzer Corps firmly held the escape route north of Salerno.

The 46th Division advanced towards Nocera. The 56th advanced towards Avellino, which was taken on the 30th by the Americans who also met the left flank of the 8th Army, advancing from Potenza, at Pescopagano. Naples was entered on 30 September. Southern Italy, from Naples to the Gargano peninsula had been invaded.

Three officers of the Polish Commandos. Their badges are clearly on display. Their berets are green with the Polish Eagle insignia and all wear the Combined Operation badge on their upper sleeves. *Polish Institute and Sikorski Museum Collection*

7th ARMOURED DIVISION

11th Hussars (Prince Albert's Own)

4th County of London Yeomanry (Sharpshooters)

The Rifle Brigade (Prince Consort's Own)

The Norfolk Yeomanry, The King's Own Royal Regiment

The Palestine Regiment

The Cyprus Regiment

12th TACTICAL AIR FORCE

15th STRATEGIC AIR FORCE

COMBAT TEAM 442

2nd NEW ZEALAND DIVISION

2nd New Zealand Division

1st Canadian Armoured Brigade (14th Canadian Tank Regiment)

CANADIAN ARMOURED CORPS

The Ontario Regiment

The Three Rivers Regiment

The Calgary Regiment

**Plate XII**

The badges of the 7th Armoured Division, the Desert Rats, are illustrated in the top row, including the cap badge of the Norfolk Yeomanry, one of its anti-tank regiments.

The Palestine Regiment was part of the Jewish Brigade Group and its cap badge depicted an olive tree within a circle inscribed 'Palestine' in Hebrew, English and Arabic. The Cyprus Regiment provided pack transport units for the 8th Army.

All regiments and corps of the 2nd New Zealand Division wore the same head-dress badge, a sacrifice which did not initially meet with approval but later this badge came to be accepted as a New Zealand distinction. While the division was still in New Zealand, a system of shoulder patches was adopted, intended for brigades, battalions and other units. However, as this method of identification eventually became too complicated, it was abolished altogether. The divisional emblem was a fern leaf.

The patches of the 1st Canadian Armoured Brigade were in the shape of a horizontal diamond and, although its tank regiments were redesignated armoured regiments, the old patches with 11, 12 and 14 CTR (Canadian Tank Regiment) were retained in Italy. Often the regimental cloth shoulder title was worn instead of the formation sign, although by that time the regimental shoulder titles should have been replaced by the 'Canadian' Armoured Corps' illustrated.

General Freyberg and two Canadian officers are depicted in this plate. The brigadier wears a US made battledress, slightly different from the British and Canadian battledress. The officer on his left wears the blouse with open collar.

# 3 The 'Gustav' Line

The German Army withdrew to positions in front of their main fortified defence, the 'Gustav' Line. These positions had been pre-arranged to delay the Allies' advance. They made excellent use of geography.

Several rivers crossed the path of the Allies on both the Tyrrhenian and Adriatic sides. All bridges over these rivers were blown and the autumn rains had swollen them. The Volturno, on the Tyrrhenian side, and the Biferno, on the Adriatic side, marked the first preliminary line of resistance. Mount Massico, Mount S. Croce and the Trigno river formed another natural line of defence from west to east. The next hurdle for the Allies was the 'Bernhard' Line on the Garigliano, Mount Camino, Difesa and Sammucro to the Trigno. The 'Hitler' Line barred the Liri valley which gave access to the north.

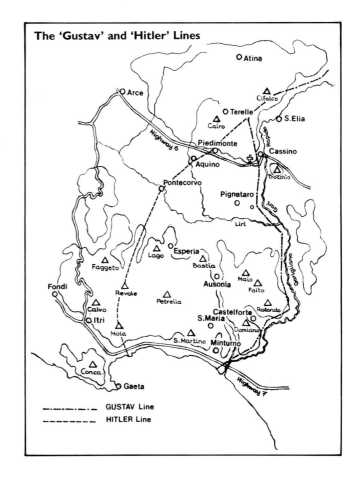

**The 'Gustav' and 'Hitler' Lines**

Atina — Arce — Cifalco — Terelle — S.Elia — Cairo — Piedimonte — Cassino — Aquino — Trocchio — Pontecorvo — Pignataro — Liri — Esperia — Lago — Bastia — Maio — Faggeto — Ausonia — Faito — Fondi — Revole — Petrella — Calvo — Castelforte — Rotondo — Itri — S.Maria — Damiano — Mola — S.Martino — Minturno — Conca — Gaeta — Highway 6 — Highway 7 — Rapido — Gari — Garigliano

—·—·—·— GUSTAV Line

———————— HITLER Line

59

## The 'Gustav' Line

The 'Gustav' Line was the Germans' main structure of defence in Italy. It crossed the peninsula in its narrowest and most mountainous region, where mountains extended from the Tyrrhenian to the Adriatic. It ran along the mountains on the right bank of the Minturno-Garigliano-Rapido, the Aurunci Mountains, Mount Cairo, Le Mainarde and along the river Sangro to the outlet of the Adriatic sea. The main river concerned flows from Le Mainarde mountains under the name of Rapido; on meeting the Gari river a mile north of Cassino it takes the latter's name. The Gari joins the Liri south of Cassino, from where the river is known as the Garigliano, which joins the Ausente farther downstream to become the Minturno.

Field Marshal Albert Kesselring, Commander-in-Chief South, was more concerned about his right flank of defence than his left because the Cassino sector controlled the routes to Rome which, being the capital of Italy, was a major political asset for both Germany and the Allies. He was well aware that any invasion had to follow one of two routes.

Highways 7 and 6 led from Capua to Rome. Highway 7 followed the low ground on the left, parallel to the sea. It was partly raised above the adjoining fields, reclaimed marshland crossed by drainage canals. A few blown bridges could have severely delayed an army's advance, even if a passage could be forced on the west of the Aurunci Mountains. Highway 6 crossed the mountains at Cassino through the Liri valley.

A second project contemplated by the Allies involved the 8th Army turning left at Pescara and heading for Rome through the Appennines. This project however, was found to be strategically unsound and was abandoned.

## The German Forces

After Salerno, all the German troops in Italy were put under command of the new Army Group 'C' which included the new 14th Army and the 10th Army. The following order of battle for the latter is shown as a basis for assessing the forces on the battlefield, but the Germans often switched formations from one sector to another and used the 'Kampfgruppe' as a combat formation.

Fred Vann, 2nd Sherwood Foresters, 3rd Infantry Brigade of the 1st Division. This brigade was initially the second but in 1945 it became the third in order of precedence; three red strips were worn under the formation sign thereafter. *F. Vann Collection*

**10th Army**

14th Panzer Corps (Tyrrhenian Sector)
  15th and 29th Panzer Grenadier Divisions
  44th, 94th and 305th Infantry Divisions

76th Panzer Corps (Adriatic Sector)
  1st Parachute Division
  90th Panzer Grenadier Division
  65th Infantry Division
  16th Panzer Division

Reserve
  13th and 26th Panzer Grenadier Division
  Panzer Division 'Hermann Göring' (incomplete)
In support
  5th Mountain Division
  334th Infantry Division

## THE ITALIANS

After the cancellation of Operation GIANT II, the King and the Italian Government were stranded in Rome. The capital was virtually surrounded by German troops, who occupied the airfields and all the important military installations. During the night following the declaration of the armistice, King Victor Emmanuel III, Marshal Badoglio and their entourage hurriedly left the capital for the Adriatic coast where they boarded vessels that took them to the region of Puglie, which was still under Italian control. On 10 September 1943, they arrived at Brindisi where an embryonic government, led by Marshal Badoglio, began to function in a climate of utter chaos. On 27 September, orders were given for the formation of the 'I° Raggruppamento Motorizzato'. On 13 October 1943, the Kingdom of Italy declared war on Germany.

The Allies did not intend to use Italian troops as fighting units but needed them in a supporting role – at Salerno and Naples, Italian units were employed in the docks to unload supplies from the ships. Italian soldiers were also organised into pack mule groups which started operating on the 'Gustav' Line.

Nevertheless, it was obvious that if Italy were to survive as a nation, it had to have an army which had proven its valour on the battlefield before the end of the war.

### Allied Military Government of Italy

A pre-arranged plan divided the Italian peninsula into nine regions under the supervision of the Allied Military Government of Occupied Territory – (AMGOT) as follows:

| | |
|---|---|
| Region I | Sicilia |
| Region II | Calabria, Lucania, Puglie |
| Region III | Campania |
| Region IV | Abbruzzo, Lazio |
| Region V | Marche, Umbria |
| Region VI | Sardegna |
| Region VII | Roma (Central Government) |
| Region VIII | Toscana |
| Region IX | Emilia |

By the middle of September 1943, the Allies had invaded southern Italy, from Salerno to the Puglie, and were moving up to the 'Gustav' Line. Therefore, according to plan, the area supervised by AMGOT was divided into Regions, which were subdivided into Compartments. Sicily became Region I; the compartments that were the Italian geographic regions of Calabria, Lucania and Puglie became Region II; the Italian region of Campania was Region III; and the territory situated northeast of the latter became Region IV.

The armistice and subsequent Italian co-belligerency altered the preliminary plans. The Allies ceded to the Italian Government the

Presentation of the Victoria Cross to Captain E. Wakeford, 2/4th Battalion, Hampshire Regiment, at Monte San Savino on 26 July 1944. *A. Voller Collection*

provinces of Brindisi, Bari, Lecce and Taranto, and later also the island of Sardinia. This territory under Italian administration was known as King's Italy.

However, as Italy was no longer an enemy nation, the parts of its territory under the Allies' administration was not technically 'occupied territory' and, therefore, the AMGOT was redesignated Allied Military Government (AMG). Sicily and Calabria became the 1st District and the area to the east, except King's Italy, became the 2nd District. These were zones of limited strategic value to the Allies and were returned to Italian administration in February 1944. Regions III and IV were lines of communication of the 5th and 8th Armies and remained under AMG control.

The Allied Military Mission and the Allied Control Commission were formed to supervise the activities of the Italian Government and the implementation of the armistice's terms.

## THE EASTERN FLANK

### 8th Army Preliminary Advance

On the Adriatic side, continuing its advance from Foggia, the 8th Army found determined German resistance on the river Biferno, south of Termoli. In order to bypass this obstacle, a commando operation was hastily planned. No 3 and No 40 (Royal Marine) Commando with the Special Service Brigade's reconnaissance squadron embarked at Bari and, in the early hours of 3 October, landed at Termoli where they overwhelmed the garrison. The 36th Brigade of the 78th Infantry Division landed by sea while units of the 11th Brigade, part of the 56th Reconnaissance Regiments and some support elements managed to cross the Biferno.

Meanwhile, the incessant rain flooded the river Biferno. Only one bridge had been constructed, too weak to take tanks. Without any tank support, the forces on the far bank were facing the arrival of the 16th Panzer Division, despatched from the other side of the Appennines. On 5 October, a Bailey Bridge was set up across the river, allowing the tanks of the Sharpshooters to intervene in the battle just in time to prevent a disaster. The Canadians entered Campobasso on 14 October and the important junction of Vinchiaturo the following day.

The 78th Division's advance continued towards the next river, the Trigno, which was waded but a vicious confrontation developed in front of San Salvo with considerable losses for the assailants. Indian units of the 8th Division cleared the valley of the Trigno, leading to Isernia. More fighting took place at Vasto and Cuppello before the advance could be resumed, hampered by the usual demolitions and sharp actions by German rearguards.

The river Sangro was reached by 9 November. The riverbed was wide but, although flooded, it could be waded and even tanks went across, their weight preventing them from being washed away by the current. A bridge-head was established by the 78th Division but at the village of Mozzogrogna the Indians were pushed back by flame-throwing tanks.

**Plate XIII**
The 1st Canadian Corps was formed in England in December 1940 and sent to Italy with the 5th Canadian Division three years later.

The badges of both formations are illustrated in this plate, including all the cap badges, some examples of formation signs and two 'slip-ons' of artillery units of 1st Corps.

All divisional formation signs were rectangular, 5 by 7.5 centimetres in size. That of the 5th Division was maroon in colour. Army, corps and brigade badges were diamond shaped. That of the 1st Corps was red.

Regimental and supporting corps' designations were often embroidered on the formation sign. Five examples of the former are shown, together with a badge of 1st Corps worn by the personnel of the Royal Canadian Army Service Corps.

The Royal Canadian Navy and Air Force used the same pattern of badges as their British counterparts. Non-commissioned officers and airmen had the initials 'RCAF' in the centre of the cap badge (see Plate II).

Canadian and British servicemen, belonging to all three services, wore also similar uniforms, including the battledress, although in the case of the latter, the Canadian pattern was of better quality than the British.

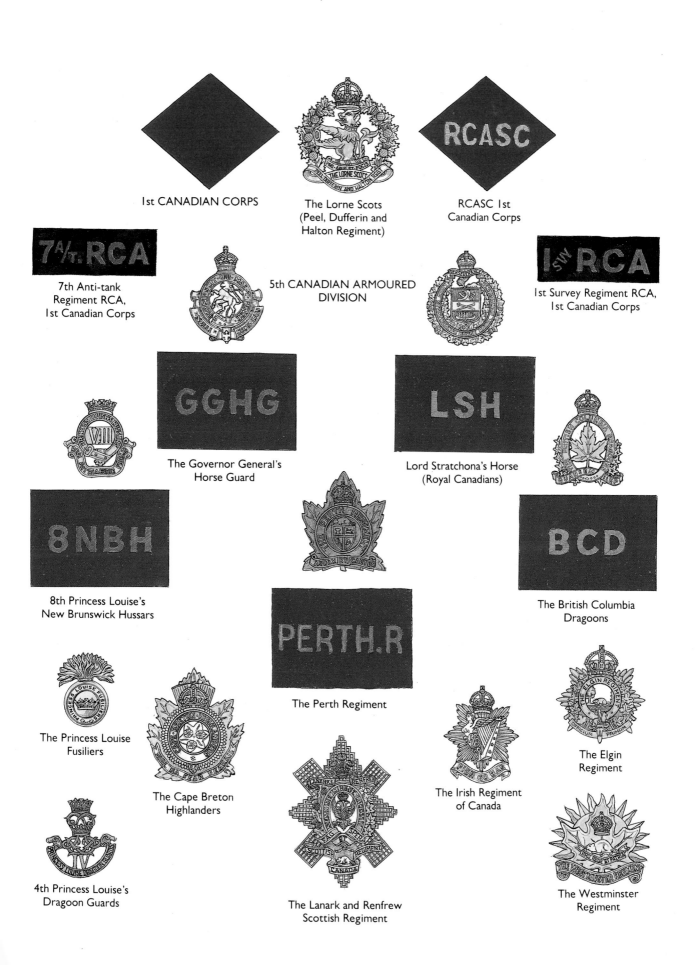

1st CANADIAN CORPS

The Lorne Scots
(Peel, Dufferin and
Halton Regiment)

RCASC 1st
Canadian Corps

7th Anti-tank
Regiment RCA,
1st Canadian Corps

5th CANADIAN ARMOURED
DIVISION

1st Survey Regiment RCA,
1st Canadian Corps

The Governor General's
Horse Guard

Lord Stratchona's Horse
(Royal Canadians)

8th Princess Louise's
New Brunswick Hussars

The British Columbia
Dragoons

The Perth Regiment

The Princess Louise
Fusiliers

The Cape Breton
Highlanders

The Irish Regiment
of Canada

The Elgin
Regiment

4th Princess Louise's
Dragoon Guards

The Lanark and Renfrew
Scottish Regiment

The Westminster
Regiment

An improvement in the weather conditions allowed air support and so made a new offensive possible. The Sangro, on the left flank of the 'Gustav' Line, was breached on 30 November. The advance continued towards the line Lanciano-Chieti, with the 78th Division on the right and the 8th Indian Division on the left.

The 2nd New Zealand Division, which had arrived in the meantime, was held in reserve on the left flank. The 1st Canadian Division relieved the 78th and the 2nd New Zealand went into action at Orsogna. After nine days of bitter fighting, the Canadians captured Ortona which German paratroopers defended house by house.

The resolute German defence combined with deteriorating weather led to the abandonment of any further activity on the Adriatic front. By the middle of January 1944, the 4th Indian Division had begun to arrive, and it replaced the New Zealanders in front of Orsogna. On the 21 January, the division was ordered to the Cassino front. The British line ran from Alfedena, to Cassoli, Orsogna and to Ortona.

---

**Picking acorns for the pigs**

'I was taken prisoner in the Western Desert and in September 1943 I was in a POW camp in Italy. We were not aware of international events but one day, surprisingly, our Italian guards packed up and left; we were free!

'I immediately scarpered towards the woods before my luck changed and after a long march, across fields and country tracks I found shelter in a farm in the mountains. Every evening I had a meal with the farmer's family and bedding in the barn but during the day I had to make myself scarce because German and fascist patrols were continuously searching the area, indeed, for escaped POWs. The farmer gave me a sack, a little food and wine and I roamed the woods all day picking acorns for his pigs.

'I met other ex-POWs in the woods, also looking for acorns, there were even Americans; obviously the entire Italian community in the area were sheltering Allied soldiers at grave risk to themselves. The Germans would have burned the farms if they knew what was going on.

'The generosity of these farmers, poor themselves, is unbelievable. If I came in this pub now as an escapee from prison the landlord would ring the police straight away.

'Months went by and one day we learned that the Allied troops were in the valley, therefore we, ex-POWs, held a meeting in the wood to decide what to do next.

'Several men reached the same conclusion: "I'm safe here, I could work on the farm. I did my stint for my country, I don't want to be put back in a unit and be killed next week. I'm staying,"'

Former Prisoner-of-War in conversation.

King George VI inspects the 2/4th Battalion, Hampshire Regiment at Monte Savino on 26 July 1944. *A. Voller Collection*

## 8th Army Reinforcements

### *The 2nd New Zealand Division*

New Zealand raised two divisions for service overseas, the 2nd for the African theatre and the 5th for the Pacific. The 2nd New Zealand Division was shipped abroad in three contingents as soon as the units were ready. The first contingent left for Egypt in January 1940 followed by the second in May, but the second went to England before rejoining the division in January 1941. The third contingent left New Zealand for Egypt in August 1940. The division saw action in Greece and Crete and later, in the Western Desert, fought at El Alamein and throughout the campaign to Tunis.

The division was initially formed by three infantry brigades, the 4th, 5th and 6th, and the 2nd Cavalry Regiment, equipped with light tanks and carriers. In October 1942, the 3rd NZ Tank Battalion joined the 4th Brigade, which was converted into an armoured formation. The conversion took place in Egypt while the rest of the division, with the 5th and 6th Brigades and a British armoured brigade in support, drove from Alamein to Tunisia.

After the end of the war in North Africa, the division returned to Egypt. As a 'mixed' division, with its new armoured brigade, it sailed for Taranto in October 1943.

### 2nd New Zealand Division

4th Armoured Brigade
    18th, 19th and 20th Armoured
      Regiments
    22nd Motor Battalion
    Forward Delivery Squadron
    Workshop and Recovery Unit REME
    Band

5th Infantry Brigade
    21st, 22nd and 23rd Infantry
      Battalions
    28th Maori Infantry Battalion
6th Infantry Brigade
    24th, 25th and 26th Infantry
      Battalions

1er DIVISION DE MARCHE D'INFANTERIE

13eDemi Brigade de la Légion Etrangère

22e Bataillon de Marche Nord Africain

4e, 5e et 11e Bataillons de Marche

4e Brigade

21e et 24e Bataillons de Marche

Bataillon d'Infanterie de Marine et du Pacifique

1er Régiment de Fusiliers Marins

1er Régiment d'Artillerie

21e Groupe Antillais de DCA

Forces Terrestres Antiaèriennes

1er Bataillon du Génie

101e, 102e et 103e Campagnie Auto

1er Bataillon de Transmissions

Ambulance Chirurgicale Légè

7e Régiment de Chasseurs d'Afrique

8e Régiment de Chasseurs d'Afrique

Régiment d'Artillerie Coloniale du Levant

17e Groupe de Forces Terrestres Antiaériennes

Ambulance Hadfield Spears

Groupe Sanitaire Divisionnaire

Groupe Sanitaire Divisionnaire No 2

1er Bataillon Médical

**Plate XIV**
Shown in this plate are all the badges worn in Italy by the 1ère Division de Marche d'Infanterie, formerly the 1st Free French Division.

The division's emblem, appropriately, was the Cross of Lorraine. A printed version of this badge was made in Tunisia in 1943. It is a sleeve insignia. The next illustrated is a collar patch of the 13th Demi Brigade of the Foreign Legion, worn on 'tenue de sortie'. Another badge with khaki background was used on field uniform.

All the other badges in this plate were made of metal and enamel, or simply metal, and were worn on the breast pocket.

As most divisional units already existed well before the formation of the Free French Division most had their own badge, some of which were made in Cairo. The badge of the Ambulance Hadfield Spears was made in England, as this unit was founded by two generous English ladies, the coat of arms of whom are depicted on the badge. It is difficult to establish how many medical units went to Italy, probably all.

The uniforms were of American pattern with French items added, képis for instance. French rank insignia was worn on the shoulder straps by officers.

The Moroccan drummer illustrated wears the 'chèche', the typical Moroccan head-dress, ornamented with coloured ribbon to identify the battalion, and cap badge, as shown on Plate XV (Tirailleurs Marocains).

## 4th Indian Division

As the political situation in Europe deteriorated in the 1930s, the British Government requested the Government of India to accept additional responsibilities and, in the event of an emergency, to designate two brigade groups for overseas service. The 4th Indian Division was created in the Deccan District as an administrative organisation for this contingency.

In August 1939, the 11th Brigade of the division arrived in Egypt, followed by the 5th Brigade and support units. The two brigades fought against the Italians during General Wavell's offensive.

At the beginning of January 1941, the 4th Indian Division, with its three infantry brigades, sailed to East Africa to take part in the war against the Italians in Ethiopia. By the end of April, after another victorious campaign, it had returned to Egypt.

The 5th Indian Brigade was sent to Syria until September. The rest of the division went to the Western Desert until early 1942 when the division was temporarily broken up, one brigade going to Cyprus, one to Palestine and another to the Canal Zone. The 4th Indian Division rejoined the 8th Army at Alamein and fought in Libya and Tunisia until the end of the war in North Africa.

Italy was the division's next assignment. It disembarked at Taranto on 8 December 1943.

**4th Indian Division**
5th Indian Infantry Brigade
    1/4th The Essex Regiment
    4/6th Rajputana Rifles
    1/9th Gurkha Rifles
    3rd (Queen Mary's Own) 10th Baluch Regiment (June 1944)
7th Indian Infantry Brigade
    1st The Royal Sussex Regiment
    4/16th Punjab Regiment
    1/2nd King Edward VII's Own Gurkha Rifles
    2 (Royal)/11th Sikh Regiment (June 1944)
    4/11th Sikh Regiment (August 1944)
11th Indian Infantry Brigade
    2nd The Queen's Own Cameron Highlanders
    1 (Wellesley's)/6th Rajputana Rifles
    3 (Royal)/12th Frontier Force Regiment
    2/7th Gurkha Rifles

Divisional Troops
Royal Artillery
    1st, 11th and 31st Field Regiment
    149th Anti-tank Regiment (The Lancashire Hussars)
    57th Light-Anti-aircraft Regiment
Royal Indian Engineers
    4th Field Company King George V's Bengal Sapper and Miners
    12th Field Company Queen Victoria's Own Madras Sappers and Miners
    21st Field Company Royal Bombay Sappers and Miners
    11th Field Park Company Queen Victoria's Own Madras Sappers and Miners
    5th Bridging Platoon Sappers and Miners
Royal Signals
    4th Indian Division
Reconnaissance Corps
    The Central India Horse
Machine-gun Battalion
    6th Rajputana Rifles

## 1st (Italian) Motorised Group

On 27 September 1943, the General Staff of the 'Regio Esercito' issued Order No 70/V for the constitution and mobilisation of the 'I° Raggruppamento Motorizzato'. This was the first formation of the new Italian Army, known in Italy as the 'Army of the South' because another army was raised in the north under the auspices of the Germans.

The most reliable units available in those chaotic days were hastily assembled together. The infantry regiment, for instance, comprised one battalion from the 67th Regiment of the 58th 'Legrano' Division, which managed to reach the Puglie from the south of France; another battalion was part of the 93rd Regiment of the 18th 'Messina' Division, from Yugoslavia; and the third battalion, the 51st 'Bersaglieri' was an officers' training unit.

At the beginning of November, the group was transferred to Avellino. A month later, it went to the front with the task of capturing Mount Lungo, together with the 36th 'Texas' Division.

**I° Raggruppamento Motorizzato**

67° Reggimento Fanteria
Reggimento Artiglieria Motorizzato
Battaglione Controcarri
Compagnia Mista del Genio

Sezione Carabinieri
Servizi: Nucleo Sanità e Nucleo
 Sussistenza

## THE WESTERN FLANK

### 5th Army Preliminary Advance

After the break-out from the Salerno beach-head, the British 10th Corps took Naples and advanced on the left flank of the US Corps, formed by the 3rd, 34th and 45th Divisions. The 10th Corps was to cross the Volturno at its lower and wider stretch, but the Volturno was in flood and the current was strong. Therefore, the Corps, under enemy fire, could not find a suitable crossing point. Several attempts were made until the 7th Armoured Division, which was supposed to mount only a diversionary attack,

Men of the 1st Battalion, 361st Regiment, 91st Division who were awarded Silver and Bronze Stars prior to the battles on the 'Gothic' Line. *R. Livengood Collection*

managed to establish a bridge-head. A Bailey Bridge was pushed through on the following day, 11 October. The 46th Division had a bridge-head on the coast and the 56th (London) crossed the river on an American bridge, in the sector of 3rd Division, establishing its own bridge near Capua on 19 October.

The 5th Army did not arrive in front of the 'Bernhard' Line until the beginning of November. On 11 November the 56th Division launched a first attack on Monte Camino. However, not until a second attempt, preceded by a massive artillery barrage, in December did the Germans decide to retreat to the 'Gustav' Line.

In the same area, the 1st Special Service Force, in its first action, captured Mount La Difesa, and later Mounts Majo and Vischiaturo. The 36th 'Texas' Division took Mount Maggiore and Mount Lungo, the latter with the co-operation of the 1st (Italian) Motorised Group, and the village of S. Pietro.

### The 5th Army at Cassino

The weary advance to the 'Gustav' Line cost a great deal of men and materials to the 5th Army. As the main battle had not yet even begun, new resources were required to guarantee a positive result in the future operations. The British 7th Armoured Division was due to return to Britain but the US 2nd Corps became available together with some new formations. A major reorganisation took place.

Lt General Clark on a visit to Polish units, accompanied by Maj. General Anders. He wears the 13th Army Group shoulder patch with five overseas service strips on his left forearm, amounting to two and a half years service abroad. His garrison cap is dark with gold braid piping, and he wears an O.D. (khaki) shirt and trousers with high-laced paratrooper's boots. *Polish Institute and Sikorski Museum Collection*

**US 5th Army**
November-December 1943
US 2nd Corps
  1st Special Service Force
  1st Armored Division
  3rd Infantry Division 'Marne'
  36th Infantry Division 'Texas'
US 6th Corps
  34th Infantry Division 'Red Bull'
  45th Infantry Division 'Thunderbird'
  2nd Moroccan Infantry Division

British 10th Corps
  46th (North Midland) Infantry
    Division
  56th (London) Division
  23rd Armoured Brigade

Reserve
  1st (Italian) Motorised Group
  US 504th Parachute Infantry
    Regiment
  3rd Battalion Rangers

Men of Company L, 363rd Infantry Regiment, 91st Division, in February 1945, near the battle front. The third man in the first row is holding a Browning Automatic rifle. *R. Livengood Collection*

In January 1944, Generals Eisenhower and Montgomery and Air Marshal Tedder were called to Britain to command and organise the forces of OVERLORD. Lt General Sir Oliver Leese was appointed to command the 8th Army. At the beginning of the month, a fresh reorganisation had taken place as part of the forces available were allotted to Operation SHINGLE, the landing at Anzio.

## US 5th Army

January 1944

US 2nd Corps
  34th Infantry Division 'Red Bull'
  36th Infantry Division 'Texas'
  Combat Command 'B', 1st Armored Division
British 10th Corps
  5th Infantry Division
  46th (North Midland) Infantry Division
  56th (London) Division
  23rd Armoured Brigade

French Expeditionary Corps
  2nd Moroccan Infantry Division
  3rd Algerian Infantry Division
  3rd and 4th Moroccan Group of Tabors
  2nd Armoured Group

Reserve
  45th Infantry Division 'Thunderbird'
  1st Special Service Force
  1st Armored Division (less Combat Command 'B')
  2nd Special Service Brigade
  1st (Italian) Motorised Group

### 1st Special Service Force

This unique, joint United States-Canadian organisation was formed on 9 July 1942, at Fort W. H. Harrison, Montana, under the command of Major Robert T. Frederick. It was trained for special operations; the first was the invasion of Kiska in the Aleutian islands, spear-heading Amphibious Task Force 9. Two out of the three regiments landed by sea, on 15 August 1943. The third was to land by parachute, but the Japanese had left the island three days earlier; no opposition was encountered. The force's next destination was Italy.

### 1st Armored Division

The division was organised at Fort Knox, Kentucky, on 15 July 1940. The two light tank regiments, the 1st and 13th, came from the 7th Cavalry Brigade. Its 69th Medium Tank Regiment was formed from a cadre of the 67th Tank Regiment. The 81st Reconnaissance Battalion came from the cavalry. The 6th Armored Infantry was originally part of the 6th Infantry Division.

In September 1941, the division temporarily left Fort Knox for a period of three months' manoeuvres in Louisiana. Back at Fort Knox, the division was reorganised. Medium and light tanks were shared between the 1st and 13th Armored Regiments. The third tank regiment was eliminated, a third armored field artillery battalion was added to the existing two and a tank destroyer battalion, the 701st, was attached to the division.

In March 1942, the 1st Armored Division moved to Fort Dix, New Jersey, then to Northern Ireland. Preparations for landing in North Africa started in October when the men went to England and Scotland for further training. Finally, it embarked for Algeria.

**Plate XV**

All the badges of the three North African divisions and of the Goumiers can be shown on one plate, because, although many badges were later made in France, very few were worn by the troops in Italy.

The regiments of 'tirailleurs', 'spahis' and artillery existed before the war, and therefore, the men who still had their badges, wore them.

Only the Moroccan Mountain Division had a cloth badge for wearing on the sleeve and a divisional breast pocket badge also. The Algerian division had a divisional breast pocket badge only, made in the shape of the figure '3'.

The Goumiers wore their own native head-dress and the 'djellaba', a colourful overcoat with hood which was often used to carry provisions. With the rest of the French Army they were provided with US Army M.17A1 helmets but many favoured their own French pattern, worn by the officers illustrated on the right of the picture. Most of the Goumiers wore the helmets they were given, while the entire Algerian division used the French pattern.

Goumiers wore on the left sleeve the number of their tabor on a light blue background, or the star and crescent emblem, while the officers' badges were embroidered in gold on a dark blue background.

## 2ᵉ DIVISION D'INFANTERIE MAROCAINE

4ᵉ, 5ᵉ et 8ᵉ Régiments de Tirailleurs Marocains

3ᵉ Régiment de
Spahis Marocains

63ᵉ Régiment
d'Artillerie d'Afrique

3ᵉ DIVISION D'INFANTERIE
ALGÉRIENNE

3ᵉ et 7ᵉ Régiments de
Tirailleurs Algériens

4ᵉ Régiment de
Tirailleurs Tunisiens

3ᵉ Régiment de
Spahis Algériens

67ᵉ Régiment
d'Artillerie d'Afrique

Goums Mixtes Marocains

64ᵉ Régiment
d'Artillerie d'Afrique

3ᵉ Compagnie de
Réparation Divisionnaire

## DIVISION DE MONTAGNE MAROCAINE

1ᵉʳ et 2ᵉ Régiments de Tirailleurs
Marocains

6ᵉ Régiment de
Tirailleurs Marocains

1ᵉʳ Régiment de
Tirailleurs Algériens

Compagnie de
Transmissions 88/84

8ᵉ Bataillon
Médical

Several units were engaged in the capture of Oran, on landing. Later, the division saw action in the area of Tebourba and Medjez el Bab and farther south at Matkar. Throughout the winter, the units of the 1st Armored Division fought on every sector of the front line, at Sbeitla, Feid Pass, Sidi Bou Zid, Maknassy, from Gafsa and El Guettar in the south in March 1943 and back in the northern sector by the end of April. At the end of the campaign, the division was near Ferryville. Ten days later, it was transferred to Rabat, in Morocco, for refitting and further training.

Italy was the division's next destination. Part of the 27th Armored Field Artillery Battalion and 'B' Company of the 16th Armored Engineer Battalion landed on the Salerno beach-head on 9 September 1943. Later, 'E' Company reinforced the engineers who built bridges on the Sele and Calore rivers and later on the Volturno.

The 1st Armored Division arrived in Italy in mid-November and assembled near Capua.

### 1st Armored Division

| | |
|---|---|
| 1st and 13th Armored Regiments | 123rd Ordnance Maintenance |
| 6th Armored Infantry Regiment |   Battalion |
| 27th, 68th and 91st Armored Field | 141st Armored Signal Company |
|   Artillery Battalions | 81st Cavalry Reconnaissance |
| 16th Armored Engineers Battalion |   Squadron |
| 47th Armored Medical Battalion | |

### French Expeditionary Corps

The Vichy Government was hostile towards the Allies and had formally declared that it would resist any attack on its colonial possessions, a declaration implemented at Dakar, in Syria and Madagascar. Equally, although half-heartedly, its forces opposed the Allied landing in North Africa, until 11 November when all resistance ended by order of Admiral Jean Darlan, the commander of the French armed forces and member of the Vichy Government in North Africa. Later, the French joined the Allies' cause and a new French Army was formed, partly equipped with American materials.

At the beginning of 1943, three divisions in Algeria and two in Morocco were constituted, and the Free French Division was formed by reorganising two Free French Brigades and other units. The new army was composed of veteran Free French combatants and ex-Vichy soldiers who obviously had little in common. The north African colonial troops had their own nationalistic fervour: a Moroccan proverb says that a Moroccan man is a lion, an Algerian man is a man and a Tunisian man is a woman. It was unwise to mix these troops together. Once they had become part of the Allied Forces, the French had to prove their own worthiness – and Allied armies in Italy were short of troops.

The French Expeditionary Corps was originally designated 1ère Armée Française which could have caused problems with HQ US 5th Army, to which the French army was subordinated. Therefore, General Alphonse Juin, the French commander, decided to

Staff Sergeant W. T. 'Jack' Sansom, Company G, 361st Regiment, at Marina di Pisa, in fatigue dress. *R. Livengood Collection*

72

redesignate his force the Corps Expéditionnaire Français. The divisions were transferred to Italy one by one and the corps became operational on 18 May 1943, formed by the following units plus many other units of the supporting services.

**Corps Expéditionnaire Français**
2ᵉ Division d'Infanterie Marocaine
3ᵉ Division d'Infanterie Algérienne
4ᵉ Division de Montagne Marocaine (4DMM)
1ʳᵉ Division de Marche d'Infanterie
Reserve
 Groupement des Goums
Armour
 7ᵉ and 8ᵉ Régiments de Chasseurs d'Afrique
Artillery
 Régiment d'Artillerie Coloniale du Levant
64ᵉ Régiment d'Artillerie d'Afrique
Batterie de Cannoniers Marins
17ᵉ, 23ᵉ, 32ᵉ and 34ᵉ Groupes des FTA
40ᵉ Groupe Colonial des Forces Terrestres Antiaériennes (FTA)
Engineers
 101ᵉ Régiment du Génie
 180ᵉ Bataillon du Génie
 201ᵉ and 202ᵉ Régiments de Pionniers

### 1ʳᵉ Division de Marche d'Infanterie

The 1ʳᵉ Division Française Libre was formed in February 1943 out of a combination of the 1st and 2nd Free French Brigades. After a reorganisation on 24 August 1943, the division was redesignated 1ʳᵉ Division Motorisée d'Infanterie and on 1 May 1944, it was renamed, again, the 1ʳᵉ Division de Marche d'Infanterie. Nevertheless, until the end of the war the division was still known unofficially as the Free French Division. This division arrived in Italy in April 1944.

**1ʳᵉ Division de Marche d'Infanterie**
1ʳᵉ Brigade (Quartier Général n° 51)
 22ᵉ Bataillon de Marche Nord-Africain
 1ᵉʳ Bataillon de la Légion Etrangère
 2ᵉ Bataillon de la Légion Etrangère
 Compagnie Canons d'Infanterie n° 13
 Compagnie Antichars n° 13
2ᵉ Brigade (Quartier Général n° 52)
 4ᵉ Bataillon de Marche
 5ᵉ Bataillon de Marche
 11ᵉ Bataillon de Marche
 Compagnie Canons d'Infanterie n° 2
 Compagnie Antichars n° 2
4ᵉ Brigade (Quartier Général n° 4)
 21ᵉ Bataillon de Marche
 24ᵉ Bataillon de Marche
 Bataillon d'Infanterie de Marine et du Pacifique
 Compagnie Canons d'Infanterie n° 4
Compagnie Antichars n° 4
Reconnaissance
 1ᵉʳ Régiment du Fusiliers Marins
Artillery
 1ᵉʳ Régiment d'Artillerie
 21ᵉ Groupe des Forces Terrestres Antiaériennes (FTA)
Engineers
 1ᵉʳ Bataillon du Génie
Signals
 1ᵉʳ Bataillon de Transmissions
Transportation
 101ᵉ and 102ᵉ Compagnies Auto
Ordnance
 9ᵉ Compagnie de Reparation
Administration
 1ᵉʳ Groupe d'Exploitation
Medical
 1ᵉʳ Bataillon Médical

### 2ᵉ Division d'Infanterie Marocaine

The division was formed in North Africa on 1 May 1943. It was the first French formation on active service in Italy, in December 1943.

73

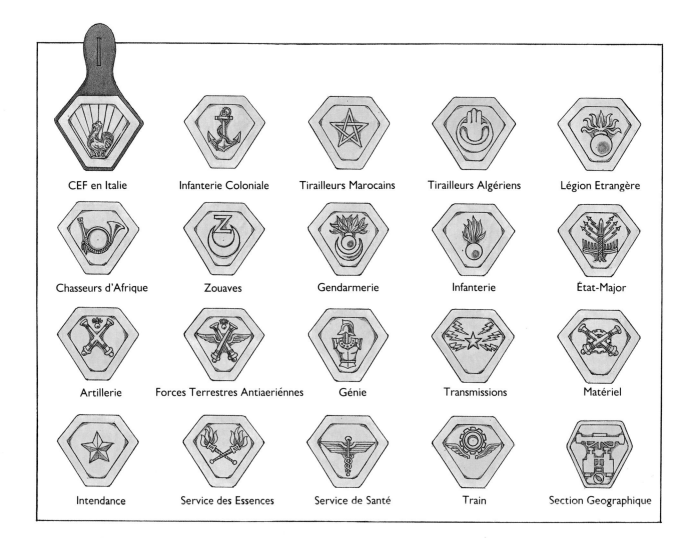

CEF en Italie

Infanterie Coloniale

Tirailleurs Marocains

Tirailleurs Algériens

Légion Etrangère

Chasseurs d'Afrique

Zouaves

Gendarmerie

Infanterie

État-Major

Artillerie

Forces Terrestres Antiaeriénnes

Génie

Transmissions

Matériel

Intendance

Service des Essences

Service de Santé

Train

Section Geographique

4th INDIAN DIVISION

6th Rajputana
Rifles

10th Baluch
Regiment

9th Gurkha
Rifles

The Royal Sussex
Regiment

16th Punjab
Regiment

2nd King Edward VII's
Own Gurkha Rifles

2nd Royal Battalion,
11th Sikh Regiment

7th Gurkha
Rifles

12th Frontier
Force Regiment

The Central
India Horse

The Lancashire
Hussars

## Plate XVI

By tradition each French unit of reasonable size has its own badge, but most units of the newly-formed divisions did not have one, nor was it possible to have enamelled badges made in North Africa.

To make up for this inadequacy, a set of brass badges was adopted in 1943. These could be worn by all as, in effect, they were branch of service badges and there was one also for the French Expeditionary Corps (Corps Expéditionnaire Français – CEF) which appeared also in painted versions (*see* Plate XIV/B).

These badges are the prototype of a new method of wearing unit insignia. Up to that time, unit insignia was worn pinned on the pocket while the new badges were provided with a leather tongue with eyelet, for attaching them to the breast pocket button. This method of attachment later became standard in the French Army.

North African troops in dress uniform wore the badge at the front of the head-dress (*see* Plate XV/A).

The badges of the 4th Indian Division are shown at the bottom of this plate. There were at least two versions of the formation sign, embroidered and printed. The regimental badges were made of metal.

### 2ᵉ Division d'Infanterie Marocaine

Headquarters
   87ᵉ Compagnie de Quartier Général
Infantry
   4ᵉ, 5ᵉ and 8ᵉ Régiments de Tirailleurs Marocains
Reconnaissance
   3ᵉ Régiment de Spahis Marocains
Artillery
   63ᵉ Régiment d'Artillerie d'Afrique
   32ᵉ Groupe des Forces Terrestres Antiaériennes (FTA)
Engineers
   87ᵉ Bataillon du Génie
Signals
   Compagnie Mixte de Transmissions 87/84
Transportation
   187ᵉ Compagnie de Transport
Ordnance
   7ᵉ Compagnie de Réparation
Administration
   9ᵉ Groupe d'Exploitation
Medical
   9ᵉ Bataillon Médical

## 3ᵉ Division d'Infanterie Algérienne

After the Allied landing in North Africa, the Division of Constantine, stationed near the Tunisian border, became a 'division de marche' under the command of General Welvert and participated in the operations that led to the liberation of Tunisia.

On 1 May 1943, it was designated the 3rd Algerian Infantry Division. After training for amphibious operations, it became part of the 1st Landing Corps. At the end of December, the division embarked for Italy where, at the beginning of 1944, it replaced the US 45th Division in the area of Venafro.

### 3ᵉ Division d'Infanterie Algérienne

Headquarters
   83ᵉ Compagnie de Quartier Général
Infantry
   3ᵉ and 7ᵉ Régiments de Tirailleurs Algériens
Reconnaissance
   3ᵉ Régiment de Spahis Algériens
Artillery
   67ᵉ Régiment d'Artillerie d'Afrique
   37ᵉ Groupe des Forces Terrestres Antiaériennes (FTA)
Engineers
   83ᵉ Bataillon du Génie
Signals
   Compagnie Mixte de Transmissions 83/84
Ordnance
   3ᵉ Compagnie de Réparation
Administration
   3ᵉ Groupe d'Exploitation
Medical
   3ᵉ Bataillon Médical

Maj. General Anders inspects the 25th 'Wielkopolski' Lancers, the reconnaissance regiment of the 5th 'Kresowa' Infantry Division. They wore white shoulder straps as a regimental distinction. *Polish Institute and Sikorski Museum Collection*

## 4ᵉ Division Le Montagne Marocaine

This formation was raised at the beginning of 1943 as the 3ᵉ Division d'Infanterie Marocaine (Marrakech), and was redesignated 4ᵉ Division Marocaine de Montagne (4DMM) on 1 June 1943. Although it was redesignated Division de Montagne Marocaine on 24 August 1943, it has always been called '4DMM'. Trained in mountain warfare in Algeria, the division was equipped according to its role with units of skiers and pack mule transport.

Units of this division participated in the liberation of Corsica from 22 September to 4 October 1943. On 18 February 1944, the 4DMM started to disembark at Naples, ready to be deployed in the Castelforte area, near the Garigliano.

### 4ᵉ Division Marocaine de Montagne (Division de Montagne Marocaine)

Headquarters
  88ᵉ Compagnie de Quartier Général
Infantry
  1ᵉʳ, 2ᵉ and 6ᵉ Régiments de Tirailleurs
    Marocains
Reconnaissance
  4ᵉ Régiment de Spahis Marocains
Artillery
  69ᵉ Régiment d'Artillerie de
    Montagne
  33ᵉ Groupe des Forces Terrestres
    Antiaériennes (FTA)
Engineers
  82ᵉ Bataillon du Génie

Signals
  Compagnie de Transmissions 88/84
Transportation
  188ᵉ Compagnie de Transport
    Automobile
  288ᵉ and 388ᵉ Compagnies
    Muletières
Ordnance
  8ᵉ Compagnie de Réparation
Administration
  8ᵉ Groupe d'Exploitation
Medical
  8ᵉ Bataillon Médical

Due to appalling casualties the 2nd and the 6th RTM were redesignated 2nd and 6th Régiments Mixtes de Tirailleurs Marocains et Algérians on 1 July and on 5 June, respectively. On 14 August 1944, the former regiment was replaced by the 1ᵉʳ Régiment de Tirailleurs Algériens and the latter reverted to its original designation, 6ᵉ RTM.

## Moroccan Tabors

Moroccan 'goums' were formed initially in November 1908 for internal security, but they could be inducted into the army during wartime. 'Goum' is the equivalent of 'company'. Three goums formed a 'tabor', battalion, and three tabors formed a 'group', regiment. The men serving in the goums were known as 'goumiers'.

Two groups plus one tabor took part in the war in Tunisia and the 4th Tabor fought later in Sicily attached to the US 7th Army. The 2nd Group of Moroccan Tabors was sent to Corsica and later participated in Operation BRASSARD, the invasion of Elba.

At the end of November 1943, the 4th Group of Moroccan Tabors went to Italy, followed by the 3rd in December and the 1st in April 1944. These three groups and the Moroccan Mountain Division formed the Mountain Corps which in May broke through the German lines.

In the centre, an Italian town council warden and two men of the Polish 'Skorpian' armoured regiment. The staff sergeant on the left wears the arm-of-service strip under the formation sign of the 2nd Armoured Division. *Polish Institute and Sikorski Museum Collection*

Polish cavalrymen of the 10th Hussars in Italy. This regiment wore the distinctive Austrian knot on their black berets as well as uniquely patterned yellow metal cap badges and buttons. *Polish Institute and Sikorski Museum Collection*

The tabors were never placed on a battlefield grouped all together but were deployed as reinforcements to infantry units.

**Tabors Marocains**

| Groupe | Tabors | Goums | | | |
|--------|--------|-------------------------------|-----|-----|------------------------------|
| I$^{er}$ | 2$^e$ | 51$^e$, 61$^e$, 62$^e$ | 4$^e$ | 5$^e$ | 41$^e$, 70$^e$, 71$^e$ |
| | 3$^e$ | 4$^e$, 5$^e$, 101$^e$ | | 8$^e$ | 78$^e$, 79$^e$, 80$^e$ |
| | 12$^e$ | 12$^e$, 63$^e$, 64$^e$ | | 11$^e$ | 88$^e$, 89$^e$, 93$^e$ |
| 3$^e$ | 9$^e$ | 81$^e$, 82$^e$, 83$^e$ | | | |
| | 10$^e$ | 84$^e$, 85$^e$, 86$^e$ | | | |
| | 17$^e$ | 14$^e$, 18$^e$, 22$^e$ | | | |

### Italian Forces
*1st (Italian) Motorised Group*

After its deployment at Mount Lungo, the group was reorganised and strengthened. The 67th Infantry Regiment was transferred to the 210th Coastal Division in the US 2nd Corps' area and a mixed infantry contingent was allocated to the group, as tabulated below. The group was sent to the front line in February 1944 in the area of the French Corps and later in the area of the Polish Corps, where it captured Mount Marrone. On 17 April, the group was redesignated 'Corpo Italiano di Liberazione'.

**I° Raggruppamento Motorizzato**
6 March 1944

Infantry
    68° Reggimento Fanteria
    4° Reggimento Bersaglieri (29° e
        33° Battaglione)
    I° Battaglione Arditi
    185° Battaglione Paracadutisti
    Plotone Rocciatori e Sciatori Alpini
Artillery
    11° Reggimento Artiglieria
      I Gruppo da 105/28
      II Gruppo da 100/22
      III Gruppo da 75/18
      IV Gruppo da 75/18
      263ª Batteria da 20

Engineers
    51° Battaglione Misto Genio
Medical
    51ª Sezione Sanità
    244° e 866° Ospedale da Campo
    34° Nucleo Chirurgico
Transportation
    250° Autogruppo Misto
    250° Reparto Salmerie
Supply
    51ª Sezione Sussistenza
MP
    39ª e 51ª Sezione Carabinieri Reali

## CASSINO

After the battle for the Mignano gap and Montelungo, which ended on 18 December with the capture of S. Pietro, no further progress was possible. Therefore, a massive attack was prepared to smash the German defences along the whole line. The French troops were deployed on the mountainous right flank, the US 2nd Corps in the centre and the British 10th Corps on the left.

### The First Offensive
The offensive started on 4–5 January 1944. The French penetrated through the hills to the north-west of Filignano, captured

Aquafondata and proceeded towards Atina, threatening the German positions from the north, barely four miles from Cassino.

In the American sector, Task Force Allen, spearheaded by the 6th Armored Infantry Regiment from the US 1st Armored Division, assaulted Mount Porchia on 4 January. The mountain was captured, lost, and recaptured time after time until 9 January when it was securely in American hands.

The 141st Regiment of the 'Texas' Division relieved the 6th of Task Force Allen on Mount Porchia. On 15 January, together with the 135th of the 'Red Bulls', the 141st attacked Mount Trocchio and reached the Rapido after a twenty-four-hour battle.

During the night of 20–21 January, two regiments of the 36th Division attempted to cross the river in rubber boats but only a few men managed to reach the far bank. Another crossing was attempted on the evening of the 21 January. More infantrymen went across, mainly on improvised foot bridges but the Germans opened up a fierce barrage of fire and no more troops could be put across, nor could the men on the far bank return.

10th Corps crossed the Garigliano on 17 January, with the 5th Division on the left towards Minturno, the 56th to Mount Damiano and Castelforte, and No 40 (Royal Marine) Commando and a Polish commando as reinforcements. Some troops were also landed from the sea north of the river's mouth, under supporting fire from warships.

A second American assault forced the Rapido to the north of Cassino and, while the 36th Division advanced southwards along the river, the 34th attacked the mountain defences in an attempt to capture the Abbey of Montecassino from the rear. Although it almost reached its objective, in the face of the fiercest German counter-attacks and foul weather, the offensive ended. The 36th Division reached the outskirts of Cassino town by the beginning of February.

## The New Zealand Corps

To exploit the success gained, more troops were necessary. Three divisions were transferred from the Adriatic sector, the 2nd New Zealand Division, the 4th Indian Division and the 78th Infantry Division, which on arrival formed the New Zealand Corps.

The Indians and New Zealanders replaced the Americans in the lines and, before the new offensive, on 15 February, the abbey was destroyed by air bombardment. A major assault followed, supported by a massive artillery barrage but the offensive withered a few hundred yards from its objectives.

A new assault had to be launched on 24 February from the town of Cassino directly up the slopes of 'Monastery Hill' which was the key position of the frontline while an armoured brigade would try to enter the Liri valley from Cassino. The deterioration of the weather led to the operation being postponed. During this time the defenders replaced their 15th Panzer Grenadiers with the 1st Parachute Division in the Cassino sector.

**Plate XVII**

All ranks of the Polish Army, except those of the 10th Hussars, wore the same type of cap badge made of white metal or embroidered in silver wire or white thread. The 10th Hussars (10 Pulk Huzarow) had a slightly different badge made of yellow metal (see Plate XX).

The formation signs of the main establishments are shown on this plate. The red 2nd Polish Corps' shield and title in this case are made of metal, while the same badges of 2nd Polish Corps Base are made of felt and silver embroidery, and the badge of the 7th Infantry Division is embroidered in coloured thread. There were also printed and plastic variants of some of these badges.

Four shapes of collar patches were used. Swallow-tail and triangular-shaped pennons were worn by all ranks of the cavalry, armour and by units belonging to armoured formations. Pennons were made of felt or of metal and enamel, painted metal or plastic. The rest of the army used diamond-shaped felt patches which fitted on the pointed collar of the battledress blouse and of the greatcoat, or pentagonal versions which fitted on the collar of the service dress jacket.

The wearing of beret insignia, often one collar patch or specially made badge, placed after the eagle was a characteristic of 2nd Corps only, because in shirtsleeve order no other unit badges were worn.

Some of the badges illustrated were worn on the breast pocket. Breast badges, collar badges and cap badges can be identified in the plates.

Kompania Ochrony
Sztabu 2 Korpusu

2 KORPUS

Armia Polska

BAZA 2 KORPUSU

12 Pułk Ułanów Podolskich

Znak Pancerny

Ośrodek Wyszkolenia
Br. Pancernej

Szkoła Podchorążych
Kawalerii Pancernej
Im.Gen.W.Andersa

7 DYWIZJA
PIECHOTY

Kawaleria

Pułk 7 Pancerny

2 Korpus

Generałowie

Weterynarze

Piechota

Słuzba Pieniężna

Kapelani
Wyznania Prawastawnego

Grupa
Administracyjna
PWSK

Lekárze

Audytorzy

Kapelani Wyznania
Ewangielickiego

Grupa Oświatowa
PWSK

Farmaceuci

Kapelani Wyznania
Rzymsko-Katolickiego

Słuzba Uzbrojenia

Grupa Sanitarna
PWSK

Dentyści

Kapelani Wyznania
Rzymsko-Katolickiego

318 Kompania
Kantyn Pólowych

Oficerowie
Dyplomowani

## Third Battle of Cassino

On 15 March, in the morning, Cassino was hit by an air bombardment which was followed by the Indian and New Zealand infantry attack. An unrelenting battle went on for days without any spectacular results: positions were taken, then lost. On 26 March, the 5th and 7th Indian Brigades were relieved by the 11th of 78th Division. In six weeks of combat, 4,000 men of the 4th Indian Division were killed or wounded.

The debris and rubble caused by the air bombardment obstructed the advance of the New Zealand armoured brigade which, in any case, was under constant German observation from the higher ground. The infantry was unable to capture 'Monastery Hill' either from the direction of Cassino or from the rear.

Yet more infantry was necessary and the entire Italian sector had to be reorganised. Fortunately, the Germans remained unaware of these changes because Allied air superiority denied the Germans photo-reconnaissance capability.

An Italian sergeant of a combat group wearing British Army battledress and equipment, and Italian army insignia. In the background, on the left in the same vehicle, a man is wearing an Italian forage cap. *Polish Institute and Sikorski Museum Collection*

---

### How I fed the troops

'Not only was I a pilot serving with No 600 Squadron, Beaufighter, in Italy, but I was also detailed to be in charge of messing.

'Under normal circumstances, this would have entailed very little effort but we were living under canvas, "on the battlefield", and so I was called upon to supplement our meagre rations with whatever I could forage by way of fresh vegetables, eggs, chickens and anything else I could lay my hands on.

'Corporal Harris, a cook and a farmer's son, had attached himself to me earlier on, soon after he had arrived in North Africa. He enjoyed my expeditions and we shared many an adventure in the common cause. But it was when we arrived in Italy that he excelled himself.

'At Montecorvino, our base near Salerno, we decided to establish a small farm and we commenced with the purchase of a few scrawny chickens and turkeys which we expected to fatten up on cookhouse swill. This was not enough for Harris. He had spotted a number of emaciated pigs in a local field and he persuaded me that they were just what we needed for Christmas dinner, as we had a few weeks in which to fatten them.

'The owner of the pigs readily agreed to sell four of them at what seemed a bargain price. "There they are", he said after the bargain was struck, "now catch them!" And burst into laughter.

'It was soon apparent that a starvation diet had served to improve their athletic performance and only after a long pursuit did we manage to run them, and ourselves, to earth. The farmer was still laughing.

'Back at our camp, in a makeshift sty, our purchases were soon gorging contentedly. Some days later Harris came to me with the alarming news that all our pigs proved to be boars and that, due to the improved diet their vigour had risen to the point of embarassment. To avoid a porcine gay community in our midst I decided on immediate action.

'Harris, as a farmer's son, was experienced in the various operating techniques which we discussed with our medical officer, the nearest we could find to a vet. In view of his experience, Harris was nominated for the task, with the doc in assistance, with a large bottle of antiseptic.

'The pigs' recovery was almost immediate and in no time at all they were eating heartily as if nothing had happened.

'Before Christmas, Harris was in action again but with a tear in his eyes as he had somehow gained an affection for his charges. I did not witness the event being away on detachment but I was assured it was humanely performed and with expertise.

'Alas, Christmas dinner was a disaster. The turkeys were extremely tough, the pigs were just a mass of fat. As an alternative we were compelled to make a humiliating return to bully-beef, hard biscuits and canned stew.

'After this disappointment, on leaving the mess tent. I could swear that I heard the sound of familiar raucous laughter emanating from a hostelry in the nearby village.

'Could it have been our Italian farmer having the last laugh, perhaps indulging in yet another glass of Chianti from the proceeds of his sale?

'I shall never know.'

Squadron Leader A. J. A. Roberts, DFC,
No 600 (Beaufighter) Squadron, RAF.

A well-armed reconnaissance vehicle of the US 1st Armored Division. The crew still wears winter dress. *H. M. Simpson Collection*

2 Grupa
Artylerii

Szkoła Podchargżych
Rezerwy Artylerii

Znak Pilota Samolotów
Artylerii

11, 12 Putk
Artylerii Ciężkiej

Artyleria Lekka

Artyleria Konna

7 Putk Artylerii
Przeciwpancernej

Artyleria
Ciężka

Artyleria
Przeciwlotnicza

Grupa Saperów,
2 Korpusu

663 Dywizjon
Samolotów Artylerii

Artyleria
Przetiwpancerna

Artyleria
Pomiarowa

41 Batalion
Saperów Kolejowych

Znak
Łączności

Oficerska Szkoła
Topografów

10 Kampania
Mostów Saperów

Saperzy
Kolejowi

22 Kompania
Zaopatrywania Artylerii

Oddziaśy Łączności
2 Korpusu

Pózadywizyjne
Oddziały
Ratownicze
2 Korpusu

Żandarmeria

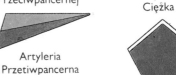

12 Kompania
Geograficzna

Szkoła
Pódchorażych Służby
Zaopatryswania i Transportu

11 Batilion
Łączności

Służba
Warsztatowo-Naprawcza

2        3

Znak Stużbowy
Żandarmerii

Stuba
Geograficzna
2 Korpusu

Kierowca
Wzorowy

Plate XVIII

The various badges of the Polish supporting corps are illustrated in this plate, starting with the branches of the artillery. The artillery observer pilots wore the eagle in flight, characteristic of the Polish pilots, with a special artillery badge superimposed upon the wreath, with green enamel leaves for those who had been engaged on active operational flights.

Several of these breast badges were adopted before the war, for instance, those of the Horse Artillery, of the Signal Corps and of the Officers' Topographic School, and even the Military Police duty badge was based on the pre-war design, although made in Italy. Others were made during and after the war, and often display commemorative dates and motifs relating to wartime events. The emblem of the 2nd Polish Corps, the Warsaw mermaid, can be seen on the badges of the 2nd Artillery Group, 11th Medium Artillery Regiment, 2nd Corps Engineers Group, 11th Railway Battalion, 11th Signal Battalion and 12th Geographic Company. The last two units displayed the mermaid on the collar badges also.

The 8th Army's shield is also shown on two of the above mentioned badges and on that of the 7th Anti-tank Artillery Regiment.

The Military Police changed collar badges twice, the second and third patterns were made of metal and enamel. The badges of the 22nd ASC Company, Artillery Supply, depicted a bear as this company had a live bear as a mascot.

The last badge on the right was worn above the ribbons by 'exemplary drivers', with red, blue and yellow backing for 1st, 2nd and 3rd class, respectively.

# 4 Operation 'Shingle', the Landing at Anzio

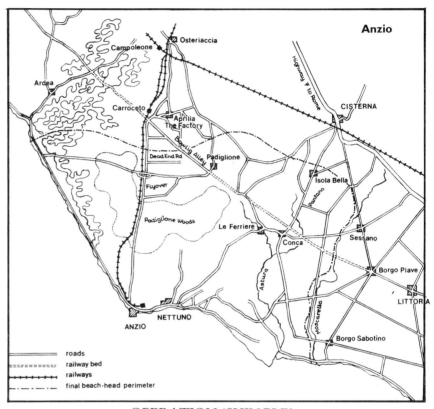

## OPERATION 'SHINGLE'

Plans for another amphibious landing on the Italian west coast had already been considered in October 1943 in order to accelerate the Allied advance. Operation SHINGLE started on 22 January 1944. It was planned to coincide with a break-through of the 'Gustav' Line a few days later, which explains the hurried offensives on the latter. The new 'Gustav' Line offensives did not achieve the expected results, jeopardising Operation SHINGLE.

The US 6th Corps at the start of the operation comprised the following:

**US 6th Corps**

US Infantry Division 'Marne'
   751st Tank Battalion
   504th Parachute Infantry Regiment
   509th Parachute Infantry Battalion
   1st, 3rd and 4th Battalion Rangers

British 1st Infantry Division
   46th Royal Rank Regiment
   No 9 Commando
   No 43 (Royal Marine) Commando

US 1st Armored Division
   6th Armored Infantry Regiment
   1st Armored Regiment

The landing operations were not preceded by naval bombardment but only by a selective shelling carried out by a British rocket-launching craft (LC[R]) with the aim of covering the noise of the approaching landing craft. No opposition was met.

Maj. General John P. Lucas, the operation's commander, was faced with a dilemma: his forces were not sufficient for an advance and, aware of the skill of the Germans in rallying in defence, he knew that if he were to leave the beach-head, his lines of communications could be severed. The invading force fanned out from the beaches to establish a defensive perimeter without encountering opposition. As there was no news of a break-through from the main front, therefore the defence perimeter was consolidated from the Moletta river to Aprilia, Conca and to the west bank of the Mussolini Canal.

German countermeasures were immediate. Field Marshal Kesselring ordered all German troops in that area to rally against the beach-head and asked the 10th Army, on the 'Gustav' Line, for support. Part of 3rd Panzer Grenadier Division, of the 'Hermann Göring', and part of the 71st Infantry Division moved northwards while 26th Panzer Division and part of the 1st Parachute Division were sent from the Adriatic sector. The 14th Army made available the 65th and 362nd Infantry divisions and part of the 16th SS Panzer Grenadier Division.

The German 14th Army took control of the new front and organised two corps for the defence in a few days. Headquarters 1st Parachute Corps had already arrived from the Garigliano sector on the day of the landing. The other German Corps was the 76th.

On 23 January, the 179th Regimental Combat Team of the US 45th Division arrived on the beach-head. General Lucas requested the balance of this formation and of the 1st Armored Division.

As German resistance stiffened, any attempt to enlarge the perimeter was firmly halted. On the night preceding the 30 January the Allies began an offensive which achieved territorial gains but also resulted in heavy casualties. The 1st and 3rd Rangers were virtually annihilated.

The 1st Special Service Force, the remainder of the US 45th Division and part of the British 56th Division were sent to Anzio in anticipation of a German counter-offensive. The German attack began on 3 February against the left flank, held by the British. More attacks followed and the positions at Aprilia (The Factory) and Carroceto were lost, together, of course, with all the ground taken during the offensive of 29/30 January.

Meanwhile, the balance of the 56th (London) Division arrived at Anzio and reinforcements strengthened the Germans from the north, allowing Kesselring to return units to the 'Gustav' Line.

In the early morning of 16 February, Operation FISCHFANG began, with *Luftwaffe* support. Its aim was to crash the defence perimeter of the beach-head through the US 45th Division which was deployed between the British 56th and the US 3rd Division.

A fierce battle raged for four days. On 29 February, a new

**Cassino** (*below right*)
This map shows the type of terrain which confronted the Allies on the 'Gustav' Line. Highway 6 and the railway ran in the Liri valley which was flanked on its north and south sides by rugged mountains stretching from the Adriatic to the Tyrrhenean seas. The sophisticated German fortifications in the Liri valley discouraged the Allies from making a direct assault there. As Montecassino was obviously the key feature of the whole defensive line, the Allies decided to envelop it from both the front and the back.

The Germans had prepared the defence of the valley thoroughly. A dam upstream on the Rapido had been blown resulting in the river valley being reduced to a lethal quagmire sown with minefields and lines of barbed wire. All trees were cut down and houses demolished on the north banks of the Rapido in order to give perfect visibility of the valley from the hills.

The 133th Regiment, with the 100th (Nisei) Battalion in place of its 2/133rd, of the US 34th Infantry Division, spearheaded the assault across the Rapido towards Points 56 and 213 on the night of 24/25 January 1944. The Americans crossed the river, were counter-attacked and went forward again. The 168th Regiment and 756th Tank Regiment joined in the battle, and later also the 135th Infantry Regiment. Meanwhile, French troops were attacking farther north.

A fierce battle developed to eject the Germans from their fortifications on the foothills, and later for the capture of the hills of Castellone and Maiola. However, the 34th managed to get through all obstacles, with its 133rd Regiment now moving towards the town of Cassino, and the other two regiments in the northern sector attempting to encircle the monastery. The advance halted in front of the defensive line running from Point 505, to Albaneta Farm and Point 593, where the Germans had built machine-gun and mortar emplacements in a naturally defensible terrain. By 12 February 1944, the 34th Division had 318 men killed and 1,641 wounded. Almost 400 were missing, presumed to be prisoners of war.

In the second attempt to break the 'Gustav' line, the 4th Indian Division was deployed on the Montecassino massif while the 2nd New Zealand Division attacked frontally through Cassino town. By 18 February, casualties were appalling.

The next offensive on 15 March was preceded by an air raid aimed at obliterating the monastery and the town of Cassino. The main effort was switched to attacking the monastery from the north-east in between the massif and the town towards Point 165, proceeding later to assault the main objective together with the New Zealanders. The 78th Infantry Division and Combat Command 'B' from the US 1st Armored Division were to strike towards the Liri valley.

Unfortunately, the destruction and debris caused by the air raid delayed the initial advance of the Allies and allowed the Germans to fortify themselves in the cellars and ruins of the town and monastery. From Castle Hill, Point 193, the 5th Indian Brigade reached the stretch of road between Points 202 and 236 but were pushed back to the road below by a German counter-attack, nor could the Germans be ejected from Cassino where they held the Continental Hotel and other positions controlling the approaches to Highway 6. During the night of the 25/26 March, Gurkhas and men of the Essex Regiment withdrew from Hangman's Hill which they had held for over a week. The 4th Indian Division lost 132 men killed, 792 wounded and 155 missing.

The 2nd Polish Corps was assigned to launch the fourth assault towards the monastery, on the top of the massif. The offensive opened on 11 May with the 5th Wilenska Brigade moving towards S.Angelo Hill, Points 706, 601 and 575, and with the 1st Carpathian Brigade against Points 593 and the Albaneta Farm. The first effort failed and a new assault began on 16 March, with the 6th Lwow Brigade on the right and the 2nd Carpathian Brigade on the left. Eventually Point 593 fell, and then Albaneta Farm, followed one by one by all the other German strongpoints.

The battle was won but the fighting continued until the last defensive positions were overwhelmed at S. Angelo and Point 575. Passo Corno and Mount Cairo were taken by the Poles on 25 May. Meanwhile, the whole 'Gustav' Line had collapsed.

offensive was launched by the Germans. Although the previous attempt had achieved a considerable success, this latter, and final, assault broke against the Allies' defences.

A period of reorganisation followed. The British 5th Division relieved the 56th, which was sent to Egypt to refit. The 24th Guards Brigade was replaced by the 18th Infantry Brigade from the British 1st Armoured Division. In the American sector, the 34th division replaced the 3rd and the 504th Parachute Infantry Regiment and what was left of the Rangers left the beach-head.

The Germans realised that they could not wipe out the Allies at Anzio and the latter realised that they could not break through while the 'Gustav' Line still existed. Both sides settled on defensive positions.

## THE BATTLE FOR MONTECASSINO

The Allied Forces on the 'Gustav' Line suffered severe losses and at the same time had had to reinforce the Anzio contingent. Therefore, new divisions were needed in order to prepare for a new offensive. Four French divisions and three groups of

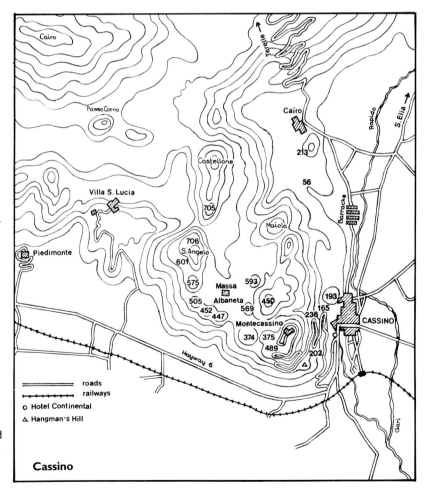

roads
railways
○ Hotel Continental
△ Hangman's Hill

**Cassino**

Moroccan tabors were available and formed the French Expeditionary Corps, commanded by General Alphonse Juin. Several other formations either arrived or were on their way to the front. They included American, British and Commonwealth troops and the 2nd Polish Corps which had been formed in the Middle East.

Before the final offensive, the available forces were reorganised. The 2nd Polish Corps was deployed in the northern sector, the British 13th and the 2nd Canadian Corps in the centre with the French Expeditionary Corps on their left flank and the US 2nd Corps along the Tyrrhenian coast.

The British 8th Army had also the 10th Corps behind the Garigliano river and the 5th on the Adriatic sector, the 6th South African Armoured Division and the 21st Tank Brigade. The US 5th Army's 6th Corps was waiting at Anzio.

The corps assembled for offensive were formed by the following formations:

### Allied Order of Battle
### on the 'Gustav' Line

| | |
|---|---|
| 2nd Polish Corps | 1st Canadian Corps |
|   3rd 'Karpathian' Rifle Division |   1st Canadian Infantry Division |
|   5th 'Kresowa' Infantry Division |   5th Canadian Armoured Division |
|   2nd Armoured Brigade |   25th Tank Brigade |
| | |
| British 13th Corps | US 2nd Corps |
|   4th Infantry Division |   85th Infantry Division 'Custer' |
|   78th Infantry Division |   88th Infantry Division 'Blue Devil' |
|   8th Indian Division |   1st Armored Group |
|   6th Armoured Division | |
|   1st Canadian Armoured Brigade | |
|   9th Armoured Brigade | |
|   1st Infantry Brigade (Guards) | |

## 2nd Polish Corps

In accordance with the Nazi-Soviet agreement for the annihilation of Poland, during the period following the 1939 invasion of Poland, the Soviets deported about 1,700,000 Poles, including women and children, deep into the USSR. After the German attack on the Soviet Union, in June 1941, the latter became a partner of the Western Alliance, which included the Polish Government in exile in London.

Meanwhile, Polish refugees, reinforced by Polish volunteers from all over the world, had already fought valiantly in the armies at Narvik, in France in 1940, in the Western Desert and, in the air, in the Battle of Britain.

General Wladislaw Sikorski, the head of the Polish Government in London, entered into negotiations with the Soviet Government to free the Poles detained in the USSR and to recruit them to form a new army. As a result, agreements were signed in July and August 1941 and two Polish infantry divisions began to be organised in the area of Orenburg. Maj. General Wladislaw Anders, himself a former prisoner, was appointed to command the new army. In December 1941, as a result of new negotiations, it

### Plate XIX
The 2nd Warsaw Armoured Division was formed in Italy by strengthening and expanding the former 2nd Armoured Brigade. The division had its own formation sign, a breast badge and divisional headquarters personnel wore pennons on the collar.

Most units of this formation by the end of the war had a beret badge as well as collar badges. Some units also had a breast badge.

The 16th Pomeranian Infantry Brigade had plain infantry collar patches (Type 1) but its headquarters and each battalion had a different beret badge made of metal and enamel. The 65th Battalion was also entitled to a breast badge which was the pre-war badge of the 65th Infantry Regiment.

The three armoured regiments of the 2nd Armoured Brigade had pennons for wearing on the collar, beret and breast badges. The 1st Lancers used the pre-war breast badge and a pennon on the beret. Similarly, all the support and service units without a special beret badge wore a left-hand side collar pennon in its place.

The Carpathian Lancers were the divisional reconnaissance regiment. They wore collar pennons, breast badge and a 3-millimetre red piping around the beret.

A knight's helmet was the emblem of the 9th Forward Tank Replacement Squadron, and was worn on an orange backing on the beret and on the collar pennons.

The 2nd Motorised Commando Battalion was part of the 2nd Warsaw Armoured Division.

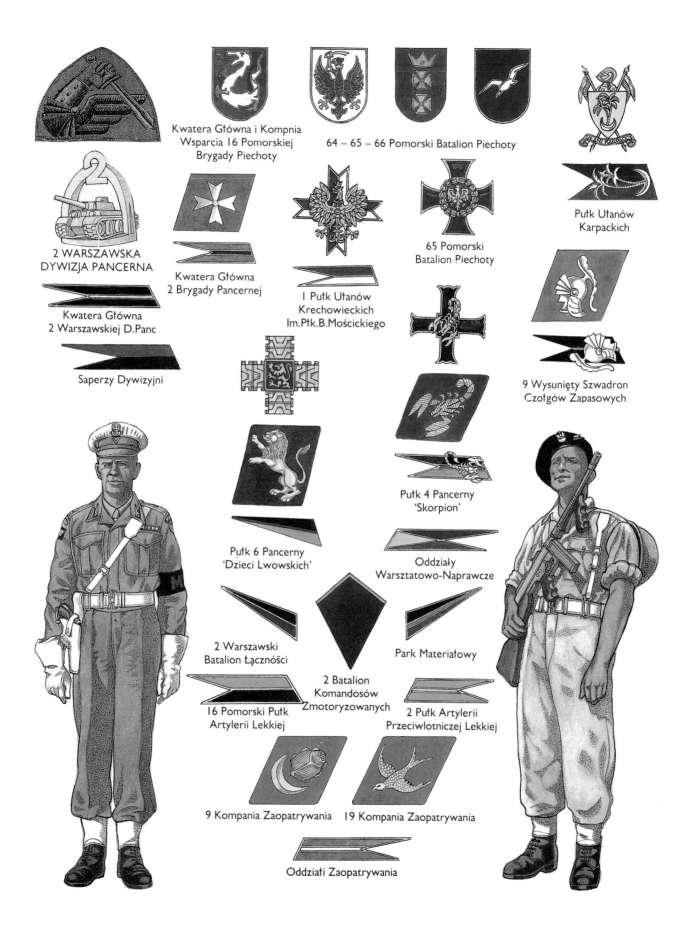

2 WARSZAWSKA
DYWIZJA PANCERNA

Kwatera Główna
2 Warszawskiej D.Panc

Saperzy Dywizyjni

Kwatera Główna i Kompnia
Wsparcia 16 Pomorskiej
Brygady Piechoty

64 – 65 – 66 Pomorski Batalion Piechoty

Kwatera Główna
2 Brygady Pancernej

I Putk Utanów
Krechowieckich
Im.Ptk.B.Mościckiego

65 Pomorski
Batalion Piechoty

Putk Utanów
Karpackich

9 Wysunięty Szwadron
Czotgów Zapasowych

Putk 4 Pancerny
'Skorpion'

Putk 6 Pancerny
'Dzieci Lwowskich'

Oddziały
Warsztatowo-Naprawcze

2 Warszawski
Batalion Łącznóści

2 Batalion
Komandosów
Zmotoryzowanych

Park Materiałowy

16 Pomorski Putk
Artylerii Lekkiej

2 Putk Artylerii
Przeciwlotniczej Lekkiej

9 Kompania Zaopatrywania

19 Kompania Zaopatrywania

Oddziati Zaopatrywania

was decided to expand the Polish Army to six divisions and also to transfer a contingent of 25,000 men to the West.

The move to Iran started on 23 March 1942. Due to ever-increasing Soviet reluctance to provide supplies to the new army, which was reduced to starvation, and the Soviets' general lack of co-operation, another Polish contingent left the Soviet Union in August.

Once in the Middle East, the Poles went through a period of reorganisation and training under the designation of Polish Army in the East. The Independent Carpathian Rifle Brigade which had won fame at Tobruk and in the Western Desert, with units from the Soviet Union, became the 3rd Carpathian Rifle Division. The other formations created at that time were the 5th 'Kresowa' Infantry Division, the 2nd Armoured Brigade and the 2nd Artillery Group. In June 1943, this force was redesignated 2nd Polish Corps. The 1st Polish Corps was formed in the United Kingdom.

During July and August, the 2nd Polish Corps moved to Palestine where it participated in the autumn manoeuvres. The manoeuvres were partly held in mountainous areas in order to acquaint the troops with the terrain they would encounter after arriving at their new destination, Italy.

Units of the 3rd Carpathian Rifle Division started to disembark at Taranto on 21 December 1943. The transfer of all the Polish forces from Egypt continued until the middle of April 1944, troops landing at Taranto, Bari and Naples. The corps was followed by the 2nd Corps Base which comprised the 7th Infantry Division as training reserve, training and servicing centres, hospitals and other supporting units. The first Polish unit to see action in Italy was the Independent Commando Company, which fought on the Garigliano river.

Due to shortage of manpower, the two divisions each comprised only two infantry brigades: the 3rd Division had the 1st and the 2nd Carpathian Rifle Brigade; and the 5th Division contained the 5th 'Wileńska' and the 6th 'Lwowska' Infantry Brigade.

The rest of the divisional order of battle followed the British pattern: three field artillery regiments; one anti-tank and one anti-aircraft artillery regiment; a reconnaissance regiment – the 12th 'Podolski' Lancers and the 15th 'Poznański' Lancers in the 3rd and 5th Divisions, respectively; and all the other supporting and servicing units of the average infantry division. The corps' 2nd Armoured Brigade comprised three armoured regiments and support units.

Finding replacements for the severe casualties suffered by the corps posed a constant problem because the Polish Government's policy was to deploy the corps together. The problem was solved by enlisting Poles from POW camps – men from the Polish territory annexed by Germany in 1939 who had later forcibly been recruited into the *Wehrmacht*, and subsequently captured by the Allies.

Apart from supplementing the losses, this unconventional method constantly reinforced the 2nd Corps. A third brigade was

Not pilots, tankmen! Lieutenants Simms and Erhardt from the US 1st Armored Division on a visit to an airfield. Both wear the standard field jacket. *H. M. Simpson Collection*

formed within both infantry divisions, the 2nd Armoured Brigade became a division and a new armoured brigade, the 14th 'Wielkopolska', was formed as well as new regiments.

By the end of the war, the 2nd Polish Corps was formed by the following units:

**2 Korpus**
(2nd Corps)
Headquarters
Dowództwo 2 Korpusu
  12 Pulk Ulanów Podolskich
    (Lancers)
  7 Pulk Pancerny (Armour)
  7 Pulk Artylerii Przeciwpancernej
    (Anti-tank Regiment)
  7 Pulk Artylerii Przeciwlotniczej
    Lekkiej (Light AA Regiment)
  8 Pulk Artylerii Przeciwlotniczej
    Ciężkiej (Medium AA Regiment)
  1 Pulk Pomiarów Artylerii (Survey)
  663 Dywizjon Samolotów Artylerii
    (AOP)
Dowództwo 2 Grupy Artylerii
  9, 10, 11, 12, 13 Pulk Artylerii
    Ciezkiej
Dowództwo Grupy Saperów
  (Engineers)
  10, 20 Batalion Saperów
  11 Batalion Saperow Kolejowych
    (Railway Engineers)
  11 Batalion Łączności (Signals)
Zandarmeria (MP)
Sluzba Zaopatrywania i Transportu
  (ASC)*
Sluzba Zdrowia (Medical Corps)*
Sluzba Materialowa
  (Ordnance Corps)*
Sluzba Warsztatowo – Naprawcza
  (EME)*
Sluzba Geograficzna
  (Geographic Corps)*
Sluzba Sprawiedliwości
  (Legal Corps)*
Sluzba Pieniezna (Pay Corps)*
Other service units.

*The last seven services were included in the order of battle of all Polish formations, although not shown in the following schemes.

**2 Warszawska Dywizja Pancerna**
(2nd 'Warszawska' Armoured
  Division)
Headquarters
Dowództwo 2 Warszawskiej Dywizji
  Pancernej
Armour
2 Brygada Pancerna
  Pulk 4 Pancerny 'Skorpion'
  1 Pulk Ulanów Krechowieckich
  Pulk 6 Pancerny 'Dzieci Lwowskich'

Commandos
2 Batalion Komandosów
  Zmotoryzowanych
Infantry
16 Pomorska Brygada Piechoty
  64, 65, 66 Pomorski Batalion
    Piechoty
  16 Pomorska Kompania Wsparcia
    (Support Company)
Artillery
Artyleria 2 Warszawskiej Dywizji
  Pancernej
  7 Pulk Artylerii Konnej (Horse
    Artillery)
  16 Pomorski Pulk Artylerii Lekkiej
  2 Pulk Artylerii Przeciwpancernej
  2 Pulk Artylerii Przeciwlotniczej
    Lekkiej
Reconnaissance
  Pulk Ulanów Karpackich
Tank Replacement
  9 Wysunięty Szwadron Czolgów
    Zapasowych
Engineers
  Saperzy 2 Warszawskiej Dywizji
    Pancernej
Signals
  2 Warszawski Batalion Łączności

**3 Dywizja Strzelców Karpackich**
(3rd Carpathian Rifle Division)
Headquarters
Dowództwo 3 Dywizji Strzelców
  Karpackich
Infantry
1 Brygada Strzelców Karpackich
  1, 2, 3 Batalion Strzelców Karpackich
2 Brygada Strzelców Karpackich
  4, 5, 6 Batalion Styrzelców
    Karpackich
3 Brygada Strzelców Karpackich
  7, 8 Batalion Strzelców Karpackich
  9 Boloński Batalion Strzelców
    Karpackich
MG Battalion
  3 Karpacki Batalion CKM
Reconnaissance
  7 Pulk Ulanów Lubelskich
Artillery
  1, 2, 3 Karpacki Pulk Artylerii Lekkiej
  3 Karpacki Pulk Artylerii
    Przeciwpancernej

Four British servicemen on leave in Rome during the winter of 1944–45. The column in the background displays the Savoy Knot, an emblem of the Italian Royal House, wolves' heads and the Roman Eagle which relate to Rome's ancient history. *H. B. Stokes Collection*

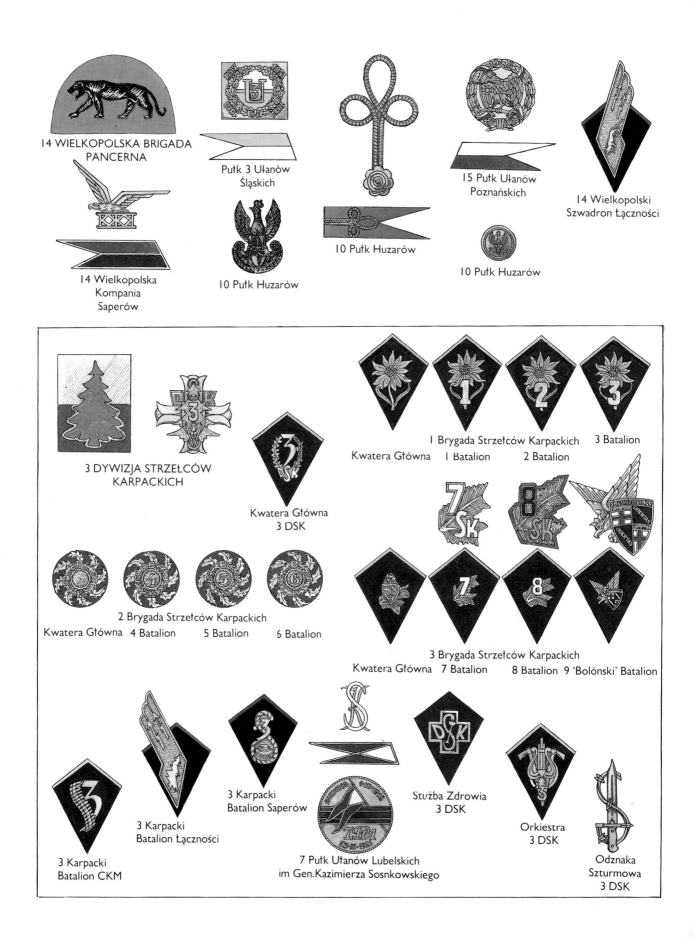

14 WIELKOPOLSKA BRIGADA
PANCERNA

Pułk 3 Ułanów
Śląskich

15 Pułk Ułanów
Poznańskich

14 Wielkopolski
Szwadron Łączności

10 Pułk Huzarów

10 Pułk Huzarów

10 Pułk Huzarów

14 Wielkopolska
Kompania
Saperów

3 DYWIZJA STRZEŁCÓW
KARPACKICH

Kwatera Główna
3 DSK

Kwatera Główna    1 Batalion

1 Brygada Strzełców Karpackich
2 Batalion

3 Batalion

Kwatera Główna    4 Batalion    5 Batalion    6 Batalion

2 Brygada Strzełców Karpackich

3 Brygada Strzełców Karpackich

Kwatera Główna    7 Batalion

8 Batalion  9 'Bolóński' Batalion

3 Karpacki
Batalion CKM

3 Karpacki
Batalion Łączności

3 Karpacki
Batalion Saperów

7 Pułk Ułanów Lubelskich
im Gen.Kazimierza Sosnkowskiego

Stużba Zdrowia
3 DSK

Orkiestra
3 DSK

Odznaka
Szturmowa
3 DSK

## Plate XX

The badges of the 14th 'Wielkopolska' Tank Brigade and of the 3rd Carpathian Rifle Division are shown on this plate. The former was formed in Egypt; it was in Italy, but never in the front line.

Both lancers regiments of the brigade wore pre-war pattern of breast badges and a collar pennon on the beret (see Plate XIX/B). The 10th Hussars wore the Austrian knot, typical of the Hussars, on the beret. Unique in the Polish Army, they wore yellow metal cap badge and buttons, which were also of different pattern to the badges and buttons of the rest of the army.

The brigade's sappers and signallers had beret badges, the latter wore the metal badge illustrated on the collar patch.

The 3rd Carpathian Rifle Division had numerous badges, most of which were adopted immediately after the war.

The 1st Rifle Brigade had the edelweiss on the collar patches and on the beret. The 2nd Rifle Brigade wore plain collar patches and the badges illustrated on the beret. The battalions of the 3rd Rifle Brigade were entitled to small badges on the collar patches, and larger versions of the same for the beret; its 8th Battalion placed this beret badge on different coloured backing according to company. The 3rd Rifle Brigade's 9th Battalion liberated Bologna, and thus was named after that city. Divisional and 3rd Brigade headquarters personnel did not wear a secondary badge on the beret.

Among the supporting units, only the signallers and machine-gunners had an extra collar badge for wearing on the beret. Similarly, the 7th Lancers wore a pennon. They also had a monogram which was displayed on the shoulder straps, and a breast badge, of pre-war pattern.

The last badge illustrated on the right is the 3rd Division's assault insignia, in gilt, silver and bronze. It was manufactured but never officially approved for wearing on uniform.

3 Karpacki Pulk Artylerii
    Przeciwlotniczej Lekkiej
Engineers
    Saperzy 3 Dywizji Strzelców
        Karpackich
Signals
    3 Karpacki Batalion Łączności

**5 Kresowa Dywizja Piechoty**
(5th 'Kresowa' Infantry Division)
Headquarters
Dowództwo 5 Kresowej Dywizji
    Piechoty
Infantry
4 Wolyńska Brygada Piechoty
    10, 11, 12 Wolyński Batalion
        Strzelców
5 Wileńska Brygada Piechoty
    13 Wileński Batalion Strzelców
        'Rysiów'
    14 Wileński Batalion Strzelców
        'Zbików'
    15 Wileński Batalion Strzelców
        'Wilków'
6 Lwowska Brygada Piechoty
    16, 17, 18 Lwoski Batalion Strzelców
MG Battalion
    5 Kresowy Batalion CKM
Reconnaissance
    25 Pulk Ulanòw Wielkopolskich

Artillery
    4 Kresowy, 5 Wileński, 6 Lwowski
        Pulk Artylerii Lekkiej
    5 Kresowy Pulk Artylerii
        Przeciwpancernej
    5 Kresowy Pulk Artylerii
        Przeciwlotniczej Lekkiej
Engineers
    Saperzy 5 Kresowej Dywizji Piechoty
Signals
    5 Kresowy Batalion Łączności

**14 Wielkopolska Brygada Pancerna**
(14th 'Wielkopolska' Armoured
    Brigade)
Headquarters
Dowództwo 14 Wielkopolskiej Brygady
    Pancernej
Armour
    15 Pulk Ulanów Poznańskich
    Pulk 3 Ulanów Ślaskich
    10 Pulk Huzarów
Tank Replacement
    14 Wysuniety Szwadron Czolgów
        Zapasowych
Engineers
    14 Wielkopolska Kompania Saperów
Signals
    14 Wielkopolski Szwadron Łączności

*Baza 2 Korpusu*

The infantry of 2nd Corps Base consisted of headquarters and four guard battalions ('A', 'B', 'C' and 'D'), the usual services including four general hospitals and miscellaneous units.

The establishment of the 7th Infantry Division which served as the Corps reserve and as the Army Training Centre are detailed below.

**7 Dywizja Piechoty**
(7th Infantry Division)
Headquarters
Dowództwo 7 Dywizji Piechoty
Infantry
17 Brygada Piechoty
    21, 22, 23 Batalion Piechoty
MG Company
    17 Kompania KM
Artillery
    17 Pulk Artylerii
Engineers
    17 Kompania Saperów
Signals
    17 Kompania Łącznosci
    Usual services, including band

**Army Training Centre**
Chief Instructor Office (Arms)
    Special Courses
    Infantry School
    Artillery School
    Signal School
    Wireless School
Chief Instructor Office (Services)
    ASC School
    Ordnance School
    EME School
    Administration School
Armoured Corps Training Depot
School of Engineering
Polish Wing CMTC

## Polish Insignia
### Formation Signs
Polish formation signs were worn on the left arm only, honorary signs on the right arm.

The mermaid on red formation sign was originally approved for Headquarters Polish Army in the East in December 1942. Following subsequent reorganisations it was to be worn by Headquarters 2nd Polish Corps and Corps Troops.

The 8th Army's shield was an honorary sign awarded by the 8th Army after the Montecassino battle. 2nd Polish Corps Order No 65, dated 12 June 1944, indicated that this honorary badge was to be worn permanently by the units that took part in the battle whether or not they remained under 8th Army's command. However, Order No 95, 17 August 1944, extended this privilege to all 2nd Corps and 2nd Corps Base formations and units.

In connection with the transfer of 2nd Polish Corps to the United Kingdom, after the end of the war, all formations were to wear the mermaid on red above their own formation sign.

**Collar Patches and Pennons of the 2nd Polish Corps, in General**

|  | Type | Colour a | Colour b |
|---|---|---|---|
| General Officers | I | dark blue* | carmine* |
| Infantry | I | dark blue | yellow |
| Field Artillery | I | dark green* | black* |
| Medium Artillery | I | dark green* | scarlet* |
| Survey Artillery | I | dark green* | white* |
| AA Artillery | I | dark green* | yellow* |
| AT Artillery | 2 | orange | dark green |
| Horse Artillery | 3 | black | scarlet |
| Cavalry | 3 | amaranth | dark blue |
| Armour | 2 | black | orange |
| Engineers | I | black* | scarlet* |
| Railway Engineers | I | black* | dark cherry red* |
| Signals | I | black* | cornflower blue* |
| Military Police | I | scarlet | yellow |
| Military Police 2nd | 3 | yellow | scarlet |
| ASC** | 2 | red | green |
| Medical | I | dark cherry red | dark blue |
| Doctors | I | dark cherry red* | dark blue* |
| Pharmacists | I | dark cherry red* | cornflower blue* |
| Dentists | I | dark cherry red* | light blue* |
| Veterinaries | I | dark cherry red* | dark green* |
| Ordnance | I | emerald green* | black* |
| EME** | 2 | black | orange |
| Geographical | I | black* | white* |
| Legal | I | raspberry red* | black* |
| Pay Corps | I | royal blue | dark cherry red |
| Chaplains | I | violet* | — |

Albert Voller, 2/4th Hampshires, 4th Infantry Division in Rome with the Colosseum in the background. Until May 1943 his battalion was part of th 46th Division, then of a Beach Group and finally it became part of the 4th Division. *A. Voller Collection*

**Women's Army Services**

| | | | |
|---|---|---|---|
| Administration | I | dark blue | — |
| Welfare & Education | I | yellow | — |
| Medical | | Jark cherry red | — |

**Notes**

*Velvet for officers

**Green and orange piping around the beret (GS cap) band for ASC and EME personnel, respectively.

The general officers wore a white metal eagle on the collar patches. Staff officers wore their own arm-of-service patches but with the eagle superimposed.

Christian Chaplains wore a different type of cross according to denomination, Catholic, Protestant or Evangelic. Jewish Chaplains wore the plain violet patch. A special cross with the Polish Eagle in its centre was made in Italy for Catholic Chaplains of 2nd Corps.

Pay Corps officers who had attended Staff College wore velvet collar patches.

Some collar patches and pennons were used by 2nd Corps only.

## British Formations
### 4th Infantry Division

This regular army division joined the British Expeditionary Force in France on 1 October 1939. During the retreat to Dunkirk, it fought on the left flank of the defence perimeter.

In June 1942, it was reorganised as a 'mixed' division, losing its 11th Brigade in exchange for the 21st Tank Brigade. In March 1943, the division went to North Africa where it entered action on 7 April at Qued Zarga and fought in the Medjez Plain and in the battle for Tunis.

In December 1943, the division was reorganised as a conventional infantry formation. The 21st Tank Brigade became a reserve formation under Allied Forces Headquarters until 3 May 1944 when, in Italy, the brigade passed under the control of the 8th Army.

On 21 February 1944, the 4th Division joined 10th Corps in Italy, and was transferred to 13th Corps on 26 March.

**4th Infantry Division**

10th Infantry Brigade
  2nd The Bedfordshire and Hertfordshire Regiment
  2nd The Duke of Cornwall's Light Infantry
  1/6th The East Surrey Regiment
12th Infantry Brigade
  2nd The Royal Fusiliers (City of London Regiment)
  6th The Black Watch (Royal Highland Regiment)
  1st The Queen's Own Royal West Kent Regiment
28th Infantry Brigade
  2nd The King's Regiment (Liverpool)
  2nd The Somerset Light Infantry (Prince Albert's)
  2/4th The Hampshire Regiment

Divisional Troops
Royal Artillery
  22nd, 30th and 77th Field Regiments
  14th Anti-tank Regiment
  91st Light Anti-aircraft Regiment
Royal Engineers
  7th, 59th and 225th Field Companies
  18th Field Park Company
Royal Signals
  4th Division
Reconnaissance Corps
  4th Regiment
Machine-gun Battalion
  2nd The Royal Northumberland Fusiliers

### 6th Armoured Division

The 6th Armoured Division was formed in the United Kingdom on 12 September 1940 with the 20th and 26th Armoured

Brigades. It lost the former in the spring of 1942 in exchange for the 38th (Irish) Infantry Brigade.

On 8 November 1942, the division embarked for North Africa as part of the 1st Army. It later engaged the enemy at Bou Arada, Fondouk and El Kourzia before linking up with the 8th Army in Tunisia. In March 1943, during the course of operations, the 38th Brigade was replaced by the 1st Infantry Brigade (Guards).

The 1st Infantry Brigade (Guards) remained with the 6th Armoured Division until the end of January 1944. On 5 February 1944, the brigade arrived in Italy where it served, temporarily under the command of several other divisions, including the 6th Armoured, until the end of the war.

The remainder of the 6th Armoured Division went to Italy in March 1944 where, on 29 May, it absorbed the newly formed 61st Infantry Brigade. The 61st Brigade had been formed in Italy on 21 May 1944 by drawing Rifle Brigade battalions, the 2nd, 7th and 10th, from the armoured brigades; the 7th Battalion derived from the 5th City of London Regiment; and the 10th, which joined the Brigade on 30 May 1944, derived from the Tower Hamlets Rifles. Although on its arrival in Italy the division comprised only the 26th Armoured Brigade and Divisional Troops, the order of battle of the infantry brigades mentioned above, the 1st and 61st, is also shown below.

## 6th Armoured Division

26th Armoured Brigade
 16th/5th The Queen's Royal Lancers
 17th/21st Lancers
 2nd Lothians and Border Horse
 10th The Rifle Brigade (Prince
  Consort's Own)
1st Infantry Brigade (Guards)
 3rd Grenadier Guards
 2nd Coldstream Guards
 3rd Welsh Guards
61st Infantry Brigade
 2nd, 7th and 10th The Rifle Brigade
  (Prince Consort's Own)

Divisional Troops
Royal Armoured Corps
 1st The Derbyshire Yeomanry
Royal Artillery
 12th Royal Horse Artillery
 152nd (Ayrshire Yeomanry) Field
  Regiment
 72nd Anti-tank Regiment
 51st Light Anti-aircraft Regiment
Royal Engineers
 8th and 625th Field Squadrons
 144th Field Park Squadron
Royal Signals
 6th Armoured Division

**Plate XXI**
Three rifle brigades were part of the 5th 'Kresowa', or 'Frontier' division, by the end of the war.

The 4th and the 6th Brigade had brigade's headquarters and battalion badges for wearing on infantry collar patches while the personnel of the 5th 'Wilenska' Brigade wore plain infantry collar patches and battalion badges on the beret. Breast badges were made for the division and for the 4th Brigade and a special formation sign for the 6th 'Lwowska' Brigade.

The 25th Lancers had a breast badge, pre-war pattern, and wore a pennon on the beret. The divisional engineers and the machine-gunners had breast badges and some support units wore the emblem of Lwow, in metal, on collar patches or pennons, as illustrated.

Apart from the badges illustrated, each formation included its normal service units whose personnel wore standard collar patches, as tabulated in Chapter Four (see Index).

Polish naval and air force personnel wore British uniforms with Polish insignia and examples of their cap badges are illustrated.

No 1586 (Polish) Flight, equipped with Halifaxes and Liberators, was at Brindisi by June 1944 and later No 318 (Polish) Squadron, flying Spitfires, arrived in Italy and was based at Rimini. No 318 Squadron had a special breast badge.

Men belonging to different regiments of the 2nd Armoured Brigade in a photograph taken in Italy. They wear khaki drill with the divisional formation sign on the right shoulder only, and the gold and blue lanyard on the left shoulder. *P. A. R. Bartlett Collection*

5 KRESOWA DYWIZJA PIECHOTY

Kwatera Główna 10 Wołyński 11 WBS 12 WBS 4 Wołyńska Brygada
4 WBP Batalion Strzelców Piechoty

25 Pułk Ułanów
Wielkopolskich

Kwatera Główna 16 Lwowski 17 LBS 18 LBS 6 Lwowska Brygada Saperzy 5 KDP
6 LBS Batalion Strzelców Strzelców

13 Wileński Batalion 14 WBS 'Żbików' 15 WBS 'Wilków' 6 Kresowa Kompania
Strzelców 'Rysiów' Saperów

Lotnictwo 6 Lwowski Pułk VI Lwowski Dywizjon 5 Kresowy Batalion
Oficerowie Artylerii Lekkiej 5 Kresowego Pułku Artylerii Łączności
Przeciwlotniczej

Lotnictwo IV Dywizjon 5 Batalion 6 Kompania
Szeregowi 5 Kresowego Pułku Artylerii CKM Zaopatrywania
Przeciwpancernej

318 Dywizjon
Myśliwsko-Rozpoznawczy
Gdański

Marynarka Wojenna Marynarka Wojenna Marynarka Wojenna
Podoficerowie Oficerowie Szeregowi

### 9th Independent Brigade Group

This formation originated from one of the brigades of the 10th Armoured Division. The division was known originally as the 1st Cavalry Division, until, in Palestine, it underwent the process of conversion to armour.

The brigade was in Syria, Iraq and Persia. In May 1942, it moved to Egypt. Later, under command of the 2nd New Zealand Division, it participated in the battle of Alamein, allocated the task of breaking through the Axis defences at Miteirya, where it suffered severe losses.

The brigade refitted in Syria and remained in the Middle East until the spring of 1944. On 28 May 1943, the brigade was redesignated 9th Independent Armoured Brigade Group. In this role, it embarked for Italy at the end of April 1944.

Privates First Class Oscar Jones and George Nelmes, medics of Company E of the 363rd Infantry Regiment, 91st Infantry Division, in field uniform. *R. Livengood Collection*

**9th Independent Brigade Group**

3rd The King's Own Hussars
The Royal Wiltshire Yeomanry
  (Prince of Wales's Own)
The Warwickshire Yeomanry
7th The Rifle Brigade (Prince
  Consort's Own)*

Brigade Troops
1st Royal Horse Artillery

1st Field Troop, 3rd Field Squadron, RE
523rd Company, RASC
166th Light Field Ambulance, RAMC

*The 7th Battalion of the Rifle Brigade, formerly 5th City of London Regiment, joined the 61st Infantry Brigade on 21 May 1944.

### 7th Armoured Brigade

This unit was formed in 1939 as a component of the Matruh Mobile Force, designated Light Armoured Brigade. It was numbered the 7th in February 1940 and redesignated the 7th Armoured Brigade on 14 April 1940.

During the winter 1940–41, the brigade participated in the first offensive against the Italians, in Egypt. In the second offensive, it was badly mauled at Sidi Rezegh and was subsequently withdrawn to Egypt.

In February 1942, the brigade was shipped to Burma, and later to India. In October, it went to Iraq where it spent the winter, moving to Palestine and then to Syria and finally to Egypt where it spent the following winter.

The 7th Armoured Brigade went to Italy on 4 May 1944 to join 5th Corps. The 2nd battalion of the Rifle Brigade was part of this formation from December 1943, but in Italy, on 20 May 1944 it joined the 61st Infantry Brigade.

**7th Armoured Brigade**

2nd, 6th and 8th Royal Tank
  Regiments

### 21st Tank Brigades

This formation was raised as the 21st Army Tank Brigade in September 1939, a Territorial Army formation composed by the 42nd, 44th and 48th Royal Tank Regiments. After some reorganisations the brigade became part of the 4th Infantry Division in June 1942. Continuing in this armoured support role, it went to North Africa in March 1943.

On joining the 4th Division, its title was changed to 21st Tank Brigade and remained unaltered until the end of the war although, in December 1943, the brigade left the 4th Infantry Division and passed under the command of Allied Forces Headquarters.

The 21st Tank Brigade arrived in Italy on 3 May 1944.

**21st Tank Brigade**
12th and 48th Royal Tank Regiments
145th Regiment, Royal Armoured Corps*

*From the 8th Battalion, The Duke of Wellington's Regiment (West Riding)

### 25th Tank Brigade

Raised in September 1939 within the Territorial Army, the 25th Army Tank Brigade comprised the 43rd, 49th and 51st Royal Tank Regiments.

In May 1940, it was reorganised as a motor machine-gun brigade but was reconverted to its original role in December. When, in June 1942, a tank brigade was assigned to the infantry divisions, the 25th joined the 43rd (Wessex) Infantry Division and was redesignated 25th Tank Brigade. In September, the brigade was assigned to the 1st Infantry Division and in November to the 54th, until the end of December.

On 2 February 1943, the 25th Tank Brigade disembarked in North Africa under the command of 1st Army and participated in that campaign as part of 5th Corps. The brigade's next destination was Italy where it arrived on 18 April 1944.

**25th Tank Brigade**
51st Royal Tank Regiment
142nd Regiment, Royal Armoured Corps*
North Irish Horse

*From the 7th Battalion, The Suffolk Regiment

Racine, Lane and Gaston, of the 1st Armored Division in an informal picture taken in an Italian cemetery. The first two men wear the tankers' field jacket, the last wears the M.1941 field jacket. *H. M. Simpson*

Officers

Infantry

Cavalry

Field Artillery

Signal Corps

Air Forces

Corps of Engineers

Armored Force

Tank Destroyer Forces

Officers

Military Police

Ordnance Department

Special Forces

Military Intelligence

Chemical Warfare Service

General Staff Corps

Inspector General's Department

Finance Department

Judge Advocate General's Department

Medical Corps

Contract Surgeon

Sanitary Corps

Nurses Corps

Dental Corps

Warrant Officers

Pharmacy Corps

Veterinary Corps

Medical Administration

Physiotherapy

Hospital Dietician

Adjutant General's Department

Quartermaster Corps

Chaplain Christian

Unassigned Officer

Army Band

Enlisted Men's US

Aide to Major General

Transportation Corps

Chaplain Jewish

WAC

Warrant Officers

Medical Corps (Enlisted Men)

## Plate XXII

Three US Army officers are shown here wearing different combinations of O.D. 'chocolate' shade and 'pink' garments, which were very fashionable during the war.

Maj. General John W. 'Iron Man' O'Daniel is seen wearing a dark garrison cap and M.1944 jacket and 'pink' – in reality light pinkish-grey – trousers, probably towards the end of the war. Eisenhower started to wear a similar short jacket, which was an improved variant of the British battledress blouse, well before its adoption in October 1944, and it was commonly known as the 'Ike jacket'.

The officer in the centre wears a more conventional combination, with pre-war jacket and the service cap. Maj. General Geoffrey Keyes, the US 2nd Corps commander, wears dark garrison cap, dark shirt and trousers.

There were other variations of the dark short jacket. For instance, the type favoured by some generals in North-west Europe resembled the pattern of the field jacket.

During the course of the war, the service (peaked) cap was declared 'limited standard, to be issued only while stocks last' and the head-dress usually worn overseas was the garrison cap, also known as 'overseas cap'.

Cap insignia and branch of service insignia are displayed on this plate. Enlisted men wore the eagle on the service cap, as did the officers but smaller and superimposed on a brass disc. Their branch of service insignia was also mounted on a small brass disc, as illustrated at the bottom of this plate.

## 5th Canadian Armoured Division

Originally formed by two armoured brigades this division was raised as the 1st and renumbered the 5th, which in 1943 became a 'mixed' division, with armoured and infantry contingents. It remained in the United Kingdom for two years as part of the 1st Canadian Army.

In November 1943, it joined the 1st Canadian Infantry Division and the 1st Canadian Armoured Brigade in Italy. The strength of the Canadians in Italy called for the establishment of a corps. Therefore, 1st Canadian Corps was sent from England and after a period on the Adriatic front, in April, the corps was transferred to the Cassino line.

### 5th Canadian Armoured Division

5th Armoured Brigade
  2nd Armoured Regiment (Lord Strathcona Horse (Royal Canadians))
  5th Armoured Regiment (8th Princess Louise's (New Brunswick) Hussars))
  9th Armoured Regiment (The British Columbia Dragoons)
11th Infantry Brigade
  The Perth Regiment
  The Cape Breton Highlanders
  The Irish Regiment of Canada
  11th Independent Machine-gun Company (The Princess Louise's Fusiliers)
12th Infantry Brigade
  4th Princess Louise's Dragoon Guards
  The Lanark and Renfrew Scottish Regiment*
  The Westminster Regiment (Motor)
  12th Independent Machine Gun Company (The Princess Louise's Fusiliers)

Divisional Troops
Royal Canadian Artillery
  8th (Self-propelled) and 17th Field Regiments
  4th Anti-tank Regiment
  5th Light Anti-aircraft Regiment

Royal Canadian Engineers
  1st and 10th Field Squadrons
  4th Field Park Squadron
Royal Canadian Signals
  5th Armoured Division
Reconnaissance Corps
  3rd Armoured Reconnaissance Regiment (The Governor General's Horse Guards)

1st Canadian Army Troops
No 1 Army Group Royal Canadian Army
  11th Army Field Regiment
  1st, 2nd and 5th Medium Regiments
Delivery Regiment
  'A', 'B' and 'G' Squadrons 25th Armoured Delivery Regiments (The Elgin Regiment)

1st Corps Troops
  1st Corps Defence Company (The Lorne Scots (Peel, Duffering and Halton) Regiment)
  1st Survey Regiment
  7th Anti-tank Regiment
  1st Corps Headquarters Signals

*Before 13 July 1944, this was the 1st Light Anti-aircraft Regiment (1st Corps Troops)

## US 2nd Corps

### 85th Infantry Division 'Custer'

After World War One, the 85th became a depot division and was reactivated on 15 May 1942 at Camp Shelby, Missouri, as part of 4th Corps. Later, it trained at Fort Young and Fort Dix and participated in the Louisiana manoeuvres. It underwent special training at the Desert Training Center before going overseas in December 1943. After a period of training in North Africa, the division took over a sector near Minturno in March 1944 in readiness for the final assault on the 'Gustav' Line.

**85th Infantry Division 'Custer'**

| | |
|---|---|
| 337th, 338th and 339th Infantry Regiment | 310th Medical Battalion |
| 328th, 329th, 403rd and 910th Field Artillery Battalions | 85th Signal Company |
| | 785th Ordnance Company |
| 310th Engineers Battalion | 85th Quartermaster Company |
| | 85th Reconnaissance Troop |

## 88th Infantry Division 'Blue Devil'

Originally known as the Cloverleaf Division, the 88th became the 'Blue Devil' after the battle on the 'Gustav' Line. During the battle, the German radio newscaster, known to the GIs as Sally of Berlin, kept picking on the Eightyeighters, describing them as 'a bunch of bloodthirsty cut-throats', once ending by calling them '. . . those blue devils!'

The division was formed at Gruber, Oklahoma, on 15 July 1942. As part of the 3rd Army, it participated in the Louisiana manoeuvres from 16 June to 23 August 1943, before being transferred to Fort Houston, Texas.

During November and December 1943, the 88th was shipped from Newport News to Casablanca, Morocco, in three echelons. After a period of training in North Africa, the division was moved to Naples in February 1944 to join 2nd Corps poised for the final assault on the 'Gustav' Line.

The 'Wild One', 1st Lieutenant Bob Benckhardt, 3rd Platoon, Company E, 363rd Infantry Regiment, 91st Infantry Division at Montecatini in November 1944. He is wearing O.D. shirt and trousers and a neckscarf – probably blue, the infantry colour. *R. Livengood Collection*

**88th Infantry Division 'Blue Devil'**

| | |
|---|---|
| 349th, 350th and 351st Infantry Regiments | 313th Medical Battalion |
| 337th, 338th, 339th and 913th Field Artillery Battalions | 88th Signal Company |
| | 788th Ordnance Company |
| 313th Engineers Battalion | 88th Quartermaster Company |
| | 88th Reconnaissance Troop |

## 6th South African Armoured Division

This division was officially formed on 1 February 1943 for service in Europe. Plans were made originally to form two armoured divisions but problems arose in finding the men and materials to raise even one. In April 1943, the South African Tank Corps regiments were disbanded and their personnel amalgamated with that of other units. Several other regimental amalgamations took place in order to build up the division. On 19 April, the division began to leave for the Middle East for training at the 6th South African Armoured Division Training Centre.

The 46th Survey Company, South African Engineer Corps (SAEC) was the first South African unit to arrive in Italy, on 8 October 1943, and joined 10th Corps. The South African Air Force was already engaged in the preliminary operations to the invasion of Sicily.

In October, an interchange of personnel began between the 6th and the 1st Armoured Division, which was still incomplete in South Africa. More reorganisations took place before the division's departure for Italy in April 1944. The Order of Battle shows its establishment upon arrival in Italy.

As the division was short of infantry, the British 24th Infantry

The 'Powder River Gang' from Company E, 363rd Infantry Regiment, 91st Infantry Division 'Powder River', at Montecatini in November 1944. Most men wear the M. 1944 field jacket and hold a can of beer, a luxury yet unknown to the Italians. Sitting are: S/Sgt Belson, T/Sgt Boker, Sgt Janetson; standing are: S/Sgt Pfeu, Sgt Rumahl, Pvt Carlin, S/Sgt Wood, S/Sgt Akers. *R. Livengood Collection*

Brigade (Guards) was attached to this formation from 20 May 1944 to February 1945 when a new South African motorised infantry brigade was formed, the 13th.

### 6th South African Armoured Division

11th South African Armoured Brigade
  Prince Alfred's Guard
  Pretoria Regiment
  Special Service Battalion Regiment
  Imperial Light Horse – Kimberley
    Regiment (Motorised Battalion)
12th South African Motorised Infantry
  Brigade
  1st Royal Natal Carbineers
  1st City – Cape Town Highlanders
  Witwatersrand Rifles – De la Rey

Divisional Troops
Armoured Reconnaissance
  Natal Mounted Rifles

Artillery
  1/6th and 4/22nd Field Regiments
  7/23rd Medium Regiment
  1/11th Anti-tank Regiment
  1/12th Light Anti-aircraft Regiment –
    South African Air Force
Engineers
  8th and 12 Field Squadron
  17th South African Field Park
    Squadron
  42nd and 622nd Field Squadrons, RE*
  166th (Newfoundland) Field
    Regiment**

*Attached on 29 June 1944.
**Attached on 18 August 1944.

## THE FALL OF ROME

The final offensive on the 'Gustav' Line was launched on 11 May 1944 on a thirty-mile front, from the mountains north of Montecassino to the sea. After two days, two divisions were across the river south of Cassino town, while the French had managed to infiltrate in the Aurunci mountains and captured Mount Faito, which was a key position of the 'Gustav' Line. In the south, the Americans took Ventosa while Indian troops were advancing up the Liri valley, capturing Pignataro on the 16th.

The Polish assault was initially repulsed on the heights north-west of Cassino but a new assault began on the night of 16 May. After a fierce battle on 18 May, the 12th Podolski Lancers reached 'Monastery Hill' and hoisted the Polish flag on the ruins of the abbey. Eight hundred men were killed in the battle.

The fall of Montecassino made an advance possible in the Liri valley. The two Canadian divisions, the 78th Infantry and the 6th Armoured Division slowly moved on, against strong German opposition.

Meanwhile, the French offensive proceeded well ahead of the rest of the Allied troops. It by-passed the next German defensive line, the 'Hitler' Line, protecting at the same time the right flank of the US 2nd Corps. The Americans captured Itri and Fondi and the port of Gaeta on 20 May.

In view of an offensive from Anzio, aimed at isolating the German forces south of Rome, the US 36th Division was injected into the beach-head. A co-ordinated offensive from the main front and from Anzio was launched on the night of 22/23 May. The Americans reached Terracina on 24 May. The following day, spearheads from Anzio met 5th Army troops near Borgo Grappa.

Cisterna fell on the same day and Artena was occupied on 27 May. In the south, the Canadians captured Pontecorvo, and Ceprano on 28 May. Valmonstone and Velletri fell on 2 June. At 9 A.M. on 4 June 1944, US Army reconnaissance units entered Rome.

**Plate XXIII**

Cap badges identified the branches of service and the class of rank of Italian Army personnel.

Generals were distinguished by an embroidered eagle, in gold or silver, according to rank. The officers in command of regiments or equivalent establishments had their badges embroidered on dark red felt, and all officers, warrant officers and sergeants wore gold-embroidered cap badges. All badges displayed a roundel, black for officers and warrant officers, and grey-green or khaki for sergeants, in which the regimental number was placed. Branches which were not divided into regiments and personnel not assigned to a specific regiment had a cross in the roundel.

All ranks below the rank of sergeant wore black machine-embroidered cap badges. All ranks were supposed to wear black cap badges when in field uniform but the officers' black badges were hand-embroidered and of a better quality than those of the rank and file.

All the badges illustrated, except those of the Alpine troops, are the small pattern for forage cap, as larger badges were worn on the peaked cap. Alpine troops wore large badges on their special Alpine hat, with feather on the left side.

The infantry of the line, parachute units, grenadiers and Carabinieri used rectangular collar patches, while the personnel of the other branches of service used cloth patches known as 'flames'. Those of the mountain troops were placed on a green backing – plain green flames for mountain infantry. Those of mechanised units were placed on a blue backing.

The shield of Savoy was worn by the personnel of the 1st Motorised Group above the left breast pocket, or above the ribbons.

Captain Russell and his men, 1st Armored Division, on the 'Gothic' Line on a sunny day of the winter 1944–45. *H. M. Simpson Collection*

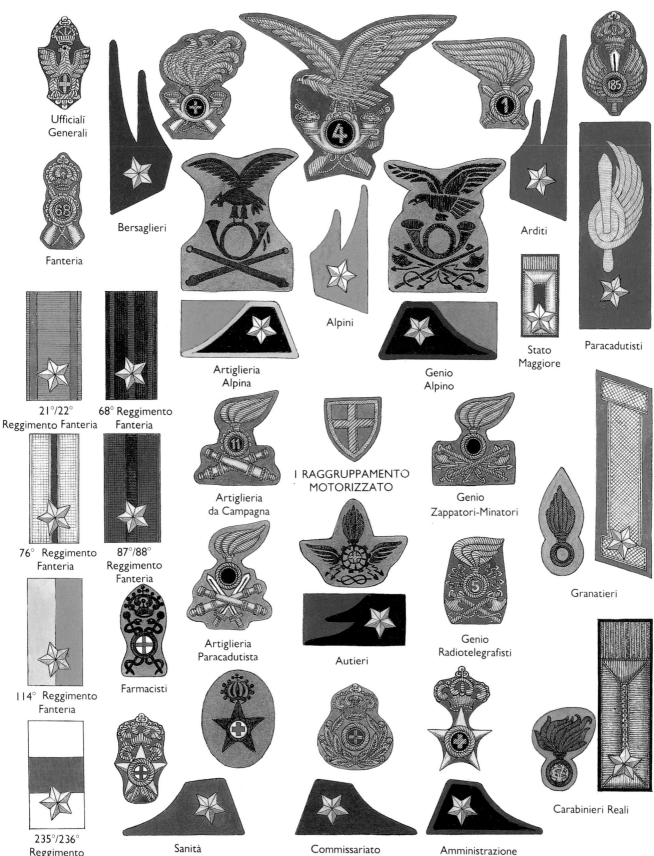

Ufficiali
Generali

Fanteria

Bersaglieri

Alpini

Arditi

Stato
Maggiore

Paracadutisti

21°/22°
Reggimento Fanteria

68° Reggimento
Fanteria

76° Reggimento
Fanteria

87°/88°
Reggimento
Fanteria

114° Reggimento
Fanteria

235°/236°
Reggimento
Fanteria

Artiglieria
Alpina

Genio
Alpino

Artiglieria
da Campagna

I RAGGRUPPAMENTO
MOTORIZZATO

Genio
Zappatori-Minatori

Granatieri

Artiglieria
Paracadutista

Autieri

Genio
Radiotelegrafisti

Farmacisti

Sanità

Commissariato

Amministrazione

Carabinieri Reali

# 5 The Invasion of Central Italy

## ALLIED AIR AND NAVAL SUPREMACY

### The Air Forces

The Allies' air power in the theatre was growing rapidly. The Americans deployed the 12th Air Support Command, which was redesignated 12th Tactical Air Force in 1944, and the 15th Strategic Air Force. The latter, however, was engaged in the combined bomber offensive on German occupied Europe.

By the end of December 1943, the British North-West African Tactical Air Forces (NWATAF) had moved innumerable units to Italy. For instance, nine squadrons were based at Grottaglie, six Kittyhawk squadrons at Foggia and four Spitfire squadrons at Campana. Over forty squadrons of different denomination were in Italy. Others were in Sicily, including South African and Australian squadrons. The headquarters of the North-West African Tactical Air Force were also in Italy, at Santo Spirito.

By June 1944, the Mediterranean Allied Air Forces were in Italy with headquarters at Caserta. Headquarters Mediterranean Allied Tactical Air Force (MATAF) was based at Caserta, Headquarters Mediterranean Allied Strategic Air Force (MASAF) at Bari, and Headquarters Desert Air Force (DAF) at Vasto. Other headquarters were still at Algiers and in Malta.

The South Africans had ten squadrons in two wings; therefore, an Advance SAAF Headquarters was formed at Bari. The Royal Canadian Air Force (Italy) Headquarters was at Portici, near Naples, although only one Canadian fighter squadron, No 417, was in Italy. No 237 (Rhodesia) Squadron, Spitfire, was based at Poretta.

The British and Commonwealth air contingent in Italy by the end of June 1944 amounted to about seventy squadrons of all denominations.

### Naval

The contribution by the Allied navies was immense. As the invasion of the peninsula progressed, the need for supplies escalated and as new ports were captured, they were immediately restored for unloading, as near as possible to the front line.

The port of Civitavecchia, for instance, was captured and, although extensively damaged, was fully operational by 9 June. By 15 June, the average daily rate of discharge through the port was 3,000 tons, rising to 4,000 and, occasionally, 6,000 tons.

The 15th Army Group had been redesignated Allied Armies in Italy on 11 January 1944. Seven days later, it had become the

Three GIs from Company M, 361st Infantry Regiment, 91st Infantry Division, wearing white parkas in the winter 1944–45. The man on the right wears an Italian M. 1891 bandolier for mounted troops with M. 1874 holster – originally the equipment of his former enemy. *R. Livengood Collection*

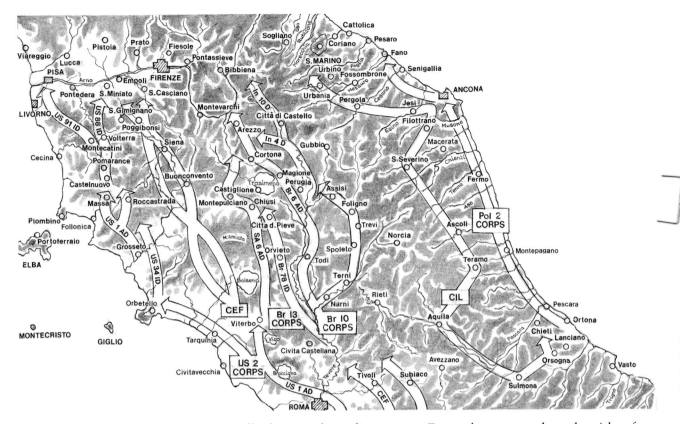

Allied Central Mediterranean Force, but reverted to the title of Allied Armies in Italy on 10 March.

## THE ARMY

Virtually three armies were in Italy by mid-June 1944: the British 8th Army, the US 5th and formations allotted to the US 7th Army, due to land in the South of France. Consequently, a large fleet was still in the Mediterranean preparing for the latter operation.

The US 7th Army was formed by the US 6th Corps, with the 3rd, 36th and 45th Infantry Divisions, the 1st Special Service Force and by the French Expeditionary Corps of General Juin. In March 1944, the British had lost the 46th and the 56th Infantry Divisions, sent to Egypt to be refitted. The 7th Armoured Division and the 4th Armoured Brigade had returned to the United Kingdom during the winter and the 201st Guards Motor Brigade followed them in April 1944. New formations arrived in Italy in due time to replace them.

Some formations had already arrived before the breaking of the 'Gustav' Line and were ready to replace others withdrawn from the battlefield in readiness for Operation ANVIL. Other divisions arrived later during the pursuit of the German forces, in an attempt to push the Germans constantly before they could be reorganised on another defensive line.

Corps' orders of battle constantly changed during this period of

105

GRUPPO DI COMBATTIMENTO 'CREMONA'

GDC 'LEGNANO'

GDC 'FOLGORE'

GDC 'MANTOVA'

GDC 'FRIULI'

FRIULI

ITALY

Ausiliari Italiani

GDC 'PICENO'

Trasporto-Rifornimento dei GDC

Reparti Portuali

5° Reparto Salmerie 'M.Cassino'

Reparti Salmerie

47th Italian Labor Battalion

Squadrone 'F'

I.

2 Regia Marina

Battaglione Alpini 'Piemonte'

Battaglione Alpini 'M.Granero'

Battaglione Alpini 'L'Aquila'

3.

4.

Reggimento 'S.Marco', Battaglione 'Bafile'

## Plate XXIV

The combat groups were formed in the autumn of 1944 and five new badges, one for each group, all on tri-colour background, were adopted. Several variants were in existence – embroidered, printed, plastic, metal, and others. One type carries the name of the group below the emblem. The transport-supply units of the groups were identified by a black and blue arm-of-service strip on the sleeves, below the group's badge.

Sleeve badges were also officially adopted for the Italian units assigned to port duties, unloading supplies, with the letters 'Tn', for Transportation, and for the pack mule groups. One of these latter groups, the 5th, adopted its own formation sign, which was made of cloth and later of metal, and depicts the profile of Montecassino.

The 'Squadron F' badge was worn on the breast pocket by an elite unit of parachutists which operated behind the German line in support of the partisans. The metal and enamel badges shown below belong to the three Alpini battalions and were worn on the left side of their cap, near the feather holder.

The 'S.Marco' Regiment of the navy was part of the 'Folgore' Group. All ranks wore a black beret with naval officers' cap badge or a brass anchor for the marines, and battledress, on which the officers had collar patches and the marines had cuff patches instead, both displaying the Lion of St Mark. There was a special arm badge for the 'Bafile' battalion, worn above the cuff patch, on the left sleeve.

The British battledress was often accompanied by old items of Italian Army dress – grey-green or newly-made khaki forage caps or Berretta holsters. Most of the badges were embroidered on grey-green background. The Bersaglieri applied their cockerel feathers on British helmets.

The men of the pack mule groups wore battledress and overcoats dyed dark green and the Carabinieri in the Allies' service retained their old grey-green or black uniforms, with the addition of a special armlet, which read initially: 'Civil Police' – Authorised by AMGOT', but 'Allied Military Government' was later substituted for AMGOT.

advance according to the situation in a specific sector. The British 1st Infantry Division, for instance, was under American control until the end of June 1944, under British 5th Corps' command in July, and under 13th Corps from 5 August onwards. The 5th Infantry Division was also under the US 5th Army command until 12 June; at the beginning of July, it was transferred to Egypt to refit, together with the 78th Division which left Italy on 17 July.

After the 'Gustav' Line and the fall of Rome, the Allies' advance began. The US 5th Army, which included the French Expeditionary Corps, advanced on the left, and the British 8th Army on the right, advancing on both sides of the Appennines.

## British Formations

### 1st Armoured Division

This division was created on 1 October 1937 under the name of Mobile Division, with headquarters at Andover and units at Aldershot and Tidworth. It went to France in May 1940 and, although still ill-equipped and below strength, it fought in the areas of the Somme and the Seine. Back in England, the division was reorganised and retrained.

In August 1941, the division was sent to the Middle East to reinforce the newly-formed 8th Army in the Western Desert. The 22nd Armoured Brigade arrived in Egypt first, on 2 October 1941. It was attached to the 7th Armoured Division, and later to other formations before returning to the 1st Armoured Division during the summer of 1942.

The 1st Armoured Division fought in the Western Desert and Egypt from May to November 1942. In September 1942, when the 22nd Armoured Brigade was attached permanently to the 7th Armoured Division, the 1st Armoured Division had received the 7th Motor Brigade in exchange. The division subsequently fought in Tunisia until the surrender of the Axis forces.

The division was redesignated 1st British Armoured Division on 5 April 1943 to distinguish it from the US 1st Armored Division. On 27 May 1944, the division was moved to Italy.

**1st Armoured Division**

2nd Armoured Brigade
  The Queen's Bays (2nd Dragoon Guards)
  9th Queen's Royal Lancers
  10th Royal Hussars (Prince of Wales's Own)
  1st King's Royal Rifle Corps
18th Infantry Brigade (formerly 7th Motor Brigade)
  1st Buffs (Royal East Kent Regiment)
  14th The Sherwood Foresters (Nottinghamshire and Derbyshire Regiment)
  9th The King's Own Yorkshire Light Infantry

Divisional Troops
Royal Armoured Corps
  4th Queen's Own Hussars
Royal Artillery
  2nd and 11th Royal Horse Artillery
  60th Anti-tank Regiment
  42nd Light Anti-aircraft Regiment
Royal Engineers
  1st, 7th and 627th Field Squadron*
  1st and 631st Field Park Squadron*
Royal Signals
  1st Armoured Division Signals

*In August 1944, the 627th Field Squadron replaced the 1st and 7th, and the 631st replaced the 1st.

## 10th Indian Division

In May 1941, not long after its formation in Ahmednagar, the 10th Indian Division was hastily sent to Iraq to secure the possession of the oilfields against Iraqi rebels. One battalion of the King's Own was flown directly to Habbaniyah airfield, sixty miles from Baghdad, while the rest was sent by sea to Basra. After the capture of Baghdad, one brigade went to Syria. Another to Iran which was threatened by Soviet Union invasion, one divisional column occupying Tehran.

Meanwhile, the situation was deteriorating in the Western Desert. In May 1942, the division was ordered to Cyrenaica where two brigades were severely mauled; the third was guarding the Egyptian frontier. Later, during the withdrawal to Alamein, the entire division was bypassed and almost overrun by the Germans but most managed to reach the 'Alamein' Line to fight for the defence of the Ruweisat ridge.

After garrison duties in the Middle East and Cyprus, the division, completely reorganised, left for Italy at the end of March 1944. A month after its arrival, the 10th Indian Division relieved Canadian troops in the Adriatic sector, near Ortona.

Three American officers of 361st Infantry Regiment in January 1945. 2nd Lieutenant Bruker wears the M. 1944 field jacket, 1st Lieutenant Larson and 1st Lieutenant Clark wear the tanker's field jacket. *R. Livengood Collection*

**10th Indian Division**

10th Indian Infantry Brigade
  1st Durham Light Infantry
  4/10th Baluch Regiment
  2/4th Prince of Wales's Own Gurkha Rifles
20th Indian Infantry Brigade
  2nd The Loyal Regiment (North Lancashire)
  1/2nd Punjab Regiment
  3/5th Maharatta Light Infantry
  2/3rd Queen Alexandra's Own Gurkha Rifles

25th Indian Infantry Brigade
  1st The King's Own Royal Regiment (Lancaster)
  3/1st Punjab Regiment
  4/11th Sikh Regiment
  3/18th Royal Garhwal Rifles

Divisional Troops
Royal Artillery
  67th, 68th and 154th Field Regiment
  13th Anti-tank Regiment
  30th Light Anti-aircraft Regiment
Royal Indian Engineers
  5th Field Company King George V's Bengal Sappers and Miners
  10th and 61st Field Company Queen Victoria's Own Madras Sappers and Miners
  41st Field Park Company King George V's Bengal Sappers and Miners
Royal Signals
  10th Indian Division

## American Formations

### 91st Infantry Division 'Powder River'

The division's warwhoop originates from a World War One incident: when asked where they were from, a detachment of Ninety-firsters yelled 'Powder River! Let 'er Buck!'.

The 91st Division was reactivated on 15 August 1942 at Camp White, Oregon, moving to Camp Adair a year later. It participated in the 4th Corps manoeuvres in Oregon. In April 1944, the 91st was sent to the Mediterranean Theatre of Operations. Its first unit to enter combat was the 361st Infantry Regiment in a sector south of Rome on 3 June 1944.

**91st Infantry Division 'Powder River'**

| | |
|---|---|
| 361st, 362nd and 363rd Infantry Regiments | 316th Medical Battalion |
| 346th, 347th, 348th and 916th Field Artillery Battalions | 91st Signal Company |
| | 791st Ordnance Company |
| 316th Engineers Battalion | 91st Quartermaster Company |
| | 91st Reconnaissance Troop |

*Combat Team 442*

This unit was constituted as the 442nd Infantry Regiment on 22 January 1943 and activated at Camp Shelby, Mississippi, on 1 February 1943 with American citizens of Japanese descent who had lived in the United States since birth. In Italy, it became an independent combat team, Combat Team 442. The regiment earned the Campaign Streamers Naples-Foggia, Anzio, Rome-Arno, North Appennines, Po Valley and Rhineland. The unit earned four Presidential Citations during the war.

For a time, it was attached to the 34th Infantry Division but, on 10 August 1944, its first battalion was reorganised and redesignated 171st Infantry Battalion. The second battalion was numbered the 100th.

This was the first regimental combat team to have its own shoulder patch, initially a round badge depicting a yellow hand holding a white sword on a blue, white and red background, the red in the centre. Later, another patch was adopted (*see* Plate XII). In 1945, this unit had a metal and enamel distinctive insignia made in Florence by Picchiani & Barlacchi.

*473rd Infantry Regiment*

Constituted on 16 February 1942 as Headquarters and HQ Company, 2nd Tank Group, this unit was formed at Camp Bowie, Texas, on 1 March 1942. On 19 March 1944, it was redesignated as Headquarters and HQ Company, 2nd Armored Group, which was disbanded at Montecatini, Italy, on 19 December 1944.

US 5th Army patrol in the north of Pracania, 7 December 1944. They are well equipped for a cold winter. *US Army*

*Miscellaneous Units*
Many other units which were not part of a formation operated independently in the Italian campaign. For instance:
15th Field Artillery Observation Battalion
75th, 548th and 985th Field Artillery Battalions
437th and 850th Signal Battalions
42nd and 972nd Ordnance Battalions
751st, 752nd and 760th Tank Battalions

## Italian Formations

*Italian Liberation Corps*
As more Italian troops became available, the Italian Liberation Corps expanded progressively. By June 1944, it included 22,000 men, with Italian weapons and equipment.

The corps was formed by two divisions (see the table). The 'Nembo' was originally a parachute division. The other division, derived from the motorised group, did not have a title and was therefore named after the commander of the Italian Liberation Corps, General Umberto Utili.

Engineers and service units of the former motorised group expanded. The medical department, for instance, included five field hospitals.

The Italian Liberation Corps was in existence for about four months but eventually became too big and was disbanded. Its components were used to form the Combat Groups.

**Corpo Italiano di Liberazione**
(27 May 1944)
Divisione 'Nembo'
Infantry
  183° e 184° Reggimento Fanteria
Artillery
  184° Reggimento Artiglieria
    I Gruppo da 100/22
    II Gruppo da 75/27
    III Gruppo da 75/13
    Batteria da 20
Engineers
  184° Battaglione Guastatori

  Compagnie Minatori, Collegamenti, Motociclisti e Servizi vari.

Divisione 'Utili'
Iª Brigata
Infantry
  4° Reggimento Bersaglieri (29° e 33° Battaglione)

4° Reggimento Alpini (Piemonte e Monte Granero Battaglione)
185° Battaglione Paracadutisti

Artillery
  Gruppo Artiglieria Someggiata da 75/13
2ª Brigata
Infantry
  68° Reggimento Fanteria
  Battaglione Marina 'Bafile'
  IX Reparto d'Assalto
Artillery
  Gruppo Artiglieria Someggiata da 75/13
  11° Reggimento Artiglieria
    I Gruppo da 105/28
    II Gruppo da 100/22
    III Gruppo da 75/18
    IV Gruppo da 75/18
    V Gruppo da 57/50
    Gruppo da 149/29

**Plate XXV**
The 1st and 4th were Regular Army divisions of the British Army. The 24th Infantry Brigade (Guards) was attached to the former division from June 1943 until March 1944 and remained in Italy to the end of the war. It later became the British contingent in the Free Territory of Trieste.

The 3rd Battalion of the Welsh Guards was part of the 1st Infantry Brigade (Guards) which operated in support of several formations, although mainly the 6th Armoured Division. It was in Italy from February 1944 until the end of the war.

The 12th and 27th Lancers and the Lovat Scouts were part of Allied Armies reserve from October 1944 onwards, joining different formations when needed. This reserve comprised armoured and infantry regiments and many artillery units, several of which were originally yeomanry regiments and perhaps still wore their original cap badge, or the Royal Artillery cap badge.

Although the blue-grey battledress (see Plate II/B) was the main Royal Air Force uniform, light khaki drill jackets and trousers were also used in Italy during summer as shown by the flying officer illustrated on the left.

Personnel of the RAF Regiment performed ground duties for the air force and were distinguished by a special cloth shoulder title.

The Brazilian Expeditionary Force was clothed and equipped by the US Army. They wore the Brazilian shoulder patch and their own rank insignia.

# THE CAMPAIGN

The two German armies in retreat had been badly mauled in the winter battles, especially the 14th Army from Anzio, formations

1st INFANTRY DIVISION

The Loyal Regiment
(North Lancashire)

The North Staffordshire Regiment
(The Prince of Wales's)

The Duke of
Wellington Regiment
(West Riding)

The Sherwood Foresters
(Nottinghamshire and
Derbyshire Regiment)

The King's Shropshire
Light Infantry

The Hertfordshire
Regiment

Royal Air Force Regiment

SCOTS GUARDS

24th INFANTRY BRIGADE GUARDS

12th Royal Lancers
(Prince of Wales's)

27th Lancers

Scots Guards

Irish Guards

Welsh Guards

Lovat Scouts

The Bedfordshire and
Hertfordshire Regiment

4th INFANTRY DIVISION

The Duke of Cornwall's
Light Infantry

The King's Regiment
(Liverpool)

The Royal Northumberland
Fusiliers

BRASIL

BRAZILIAN EXPEDITIONARY FORCE

of which had been almost annihilated. The 10th Army, withdrawing in the central sector, was in better shape and still managed to hit back hard in the Trasimeno sector.

The 10th Army's withdrawal was a prearranged, inevitable move to the next line of defence, the 'Gothic' Line where the Todt Organisation was working frantically to improve the fortifications. The longer the Allies were delayed, the stronger the 'Gothic' Line was growing.

The US 5th Army advanced along the Tyrrhenean coast towards lake Bracciano. The French Expeditionary Corps fought on its right flank.

North of Rome, the 6th South African Armoured Division captured Civita Castellana on 8 June. It met with American troops at Viterbo and proceeded towards Montefiascone, near Lake Bolsena, where it had a rough encounter with German rearguards.

By mid-June, the 8th Army's troops had reached Terni, an important railway and road junction, and advanced towards Perugia on two different roads, through Todi and Foligno. Assisi, the birthplace of St Francis, was occupied on 18 June and Perugia the following day.

Some fresh German formations were hastily inserted in the defensive lines. For example the 162nd (Turcoman) Infantry Division, made up from Russians, and the 20th *Luftwaffe* Field Division. German opposition stiffened on a line from Mount Amiata to Lake Trasimeno.

## Adriatic Sector

Meanwhile, due to the Allies' advance in the west of the peninsula the Germans were compelled to withdraw on the Adriatic sector, leaving the initiative to the 8th Army, still entrenched from Ortona roughly along Highway 84 to the mountains. As no activity had taken place in that sector for months, some formations were switched to the other side of the Appennines, and back, as in the case of the 4th Indian Division.

A cold winter day in sunny Italy. Lieutenant Vega, Captain Russell, Lieutenant Simpson and Sergeant Brumfield of the 1st Armored Division dressed according to the climate. *H. M. Simpson Collection*

General Szysrko-Bohusz confers awards on members of the Women's Army Services. Sleeve badges are sewn on the upper sleeves or on a flap which fits under the outer ends of the shoulder straps. *Polish Institute and Sikorski Museum Collection*

At the beginning of June, as the advance began, the Italian Liberation Corps joined 5th Corps on the Adriatic sector. On 15 June, the Polish 3rd Carpathian Rifle Division replaced the Indian 4th and subsequently this sector passed under the command of the 2nd Polish Corps which established its headquarters at San Vito, near Ortona. The 17th and the 26th Heavy Artillery Regiments, Royal Artillery, the 7th Queen's Own Hussars and ancillary British units were under the Polish Corps command. The 5th 'Kresowa' Infantry Division arrived in this sector between 18 and 21 June, followed by the corps' artillery and by the 2nd Armoured Brigade.

At this stage of the war, the Allies met organised Italian partisan units. One, the 'Brigata Maiella' was the first effectively to be employed on the Adriatic front in a reconnaissance role.

The Italians captured Sulmona and L'Aquila on 11 and 13 June, respectively, and Ascoli Piceno on 18 June. By the end of the month, the Allies had reached the River Chienti, south of Macerata. Geographically the area between Macerata and Ancona was aligned with the Amiata-Trasimeno line on the other side of the Appennines. Consequently, the Germans had set up a defensive line along the Chienti.

**Tyrrhenean Sector**

The rate of advance was conditioned by the congestion on the roads and by the wreckage left behind by the Germans. Occasional skirmishes with rearguards occurred but, on the western front, the Americans began to meet determined opposition near Orbetello. The French were delayed in the area of Mount Amiata and the British 78th Division and 9th Armoured Brigade became entangled in a vicious battle south of Chiusi.

**6th SOUTH AFRICAN
ARMOURED DIVISION**

Prince Alfred's
Guard

First City
Regiment

Kimberley
Regiment

Royal Natal
Carbineers

Royal Durban
Light Infantry

Natal Mounted
Rifles

Witwatersrand
Rifles

Regiment
de la Rey

Imperial
Light Horse

Pretoria
Regiment

Witwatersrand
Rifles and
Regiment de la Rey

Cape Town
Highlanders

Rand Light
Infantry

Duke of Edinburgh's
Own Rifles

Special Service
Battalion

South African
Corps of Signals

Transvaal
Scottish

South African
Engineers

South African
Medical Corps

South African
Corps of
Military Police

Technical Service
Corps

South African
Artillery

'Q' Services
Corps

Rhodesia

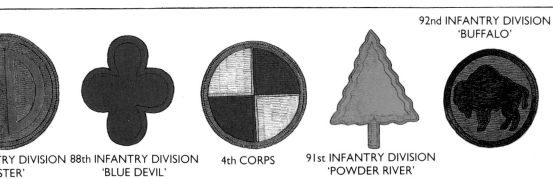

85th INFANTRY DIVISION
'CUSTER'

88th INFANTRY DIVISION
'BLUE DEVIL'

4th CORPS

91st INFANTRY DIVISION
'POWDER RIVER'

92nd INFANTRY DIVISION
'BUFFALO'

**Plate XXVI**

By the time the 6th South African Armoured Division arrived in Italy it was not uncommon for men belonging to the same unit to wear slightly different cap badges. Some wore their original South African badges, but a larger number of cap badges had been made by several Egyptian manufacturers and their quality varied considerably as a result. Some cap badges were also made in Italy towards the end of the war. Some personnel had their badge blackened or painted brown to prevent reflection.

Some regiments were amalgamated while the division was in Egypt for about a year prior to embarking for Italy and the Witwatersrand Rifles – Regiment de la Rey, for instance, adopted a metal shoulder title with the initials of the two regiments. Also, the Imperial Light Horse – Kimberley Regiment had a special shoulder title with the initials 'ILH*KR' on the same line.

The First City Regiment – Cape Town Highlanders adopted a yellow (top) and green hackle, the colours of the division. The Duke of Edinburgh's Own Rifles – Transvaal Scottish – Rand Light Infantry did not have a special badge, nor did the Natal Mounted Rifles – South African Air Force Regiment. As a general rule, all ranks continued wearing their old regimental cap badges, which are illustrated.

Five US Army shoulder sleeve insignia are shown at the bottom of this plate.

---

**'P' for Panzer**

'The sound of a heavy engine starting up came to our ears, then a puff of smoke and swirl of dust drew our attention to the tank standing beside a building in the middle distance. One of the chaps on the OP, who had been searching with field glasses, then gave a commentary. It was a Tiger, he believed, and it appeared to him that the crew were having a jimmy riddle beside their vehicle. Suddenly another tank appeared from cover on the far side of the building from the Tiger, and our companion assured us it was a Sherman. It slowly approached the building along a narrow sloping track, seemed to hesitate, started to back away, then stopped and we saw flashes coming from its gun. I think it fired three times before we heard the reports. Then the Sherman reversed back up the track and out of sight.

'A few hours later our brigade was leapfrogged and our 4.2" mortar platoon "stood down", so that we were able to examine the Sherman's handywork from close at hand. The shells from the Sherman's gun had cut through the soft walls of the building, hitting the Tiger just where the turret joined the body and lifting it off like the top of a tin of bully. By the time we came on the scene three dead German soldiers had been laid out tidily beside the turret on the road.

'We reckoned that the muzzle of the 88mm gun must have stuck out beyond the wall of the building just enough for the sharp eyes of a crew member of the Sherman to spot it before the tank backed up and fired its gun.

'We wondered if the gunner ever knew what he had done.'

Stephen Wragg, 1st Battalion, Princess Louise's Kensington Regiment (Vickers Machine-Gun and 4.2-inch Mortar Support Battalion of 78th Division)

---

The 13th Corps, strengthened by the 4th Infantry Division, attacked the west shore of Lake Trasimeno on 24 June. The 6th South African Armoured Division took Chiusi on 26 June while the British 6th Armoured Division of 10th Corps proceeded along the eastern shore of the lake. The advance was slow and costly against German units determined to hold their ground as long as possible before retreating to another position, a delaying action of which they were masters. Suddenly, at the end of June, the Germans started to retreat again.

After the Chiusi battle, the 78th Infantry Division left Italy for a period of rest and reorganisation in Egypt. The 10th Indian Division arrived in this sector. It was assigned the task of advancing along the valley of the Tiber towards Città di Castello, followed by the 4th Indian Division which turned into the valley of the River Nestore. The objective was to dislodge the Germans from the mountains south of Arezzo. Both divisions became engaged in a slow march through the mountains, stubbornly defended by the Germans, and later secured the main road between Arezzo and Florence.

The 13th Corps was on the left flank of 10th Corps moving towards Florence from the south. The US 5th Army, with the French Corps deployed on its right advanced along the Tyrrhenian coast.

In the early hours of 17 June, a French force commanded by General Jean de Lattre de Tassigny, landed on the Island of Elba, supported by French, British and American warships and aircraft. Portoferraio fell and all organised resistance on the island ceased on the morning of 19 June. During the following night, German troops landed on the north-eastern tip of Elba but were immediately attacked and forced to re-embark after suffering severe casualties.

On 24 June, the Americans took the port of Follonica, and seized Piombino the following day. The American-Japanese 442nd Infantry Regiment fought with distinction at Follonica.

At the beginning of July, the French Corps was approaching Siena which the Germans seemed determined to defend but, threatened on their left flank by the British 13th Corps, they suddenly withdrew. The town was occupied on 3 July. Ten days later, San Gimignano and Poggibonsi fell to the French.

*'Evviva, viva i Liberatori!'* People shouting enthusiastically in the streets of Bologna on 21 April 1945. The liberators in this photograph were Italians from the combat group 'Friuli'. *Polish Institute and Sikorski Museum Collection*

## Life and death at Monterosi

'By then I was a young field officer, a major of the engineers and commanded a small but elite technical intelligence team.

'On Saturday, 1 July 1944, we watched the French and American artillery shelling the Germans who had artillery spotters in the tower of the castle of Monterosi. We were out somewhere in between and I could see them through my field glasses.

'We moved on the next day as the Teutons had been driven out and we were examining a German three-cylinder diesel tractor that had been left behind when my sergeant came down and said: "Major, Sir, there is a woman in the castle who speaks English and invites you to tea."

'This sounded most welcome and we went up to the castle where they were waiting for us with tea, cookies and toasts, and real butter on the toasts.

'This English lady explained that she had come to Italy as a young girl, fallen in love and married. Her husband was then a Senator and I thought he looked like a German, perhaps descended from the numerous Germanic invasions of Italy. Their daughter was there with her young daughter and the lady of the castle told me that her son-in-law was hiding in Siena because he was sought by the Germans.

'A priest was there also and I gave him a carton of cigarettes – I do not smoke nor did I then but I always took my daily allowance of one pack and in general gave them to my men.

'The Senator asked me if I thought that he would be punished for being a Fascist. To me he seemed a fine family man, he owned land and employed quite a number of people.

'I said: "You don't look like a war criminal to me but when your country became Fascist you were caught up in it and like a train, you cannot get off until it stops."

'Twenty years later I was driving down from Bologna and south-west of Siena I spotted the tower of Monterosi. I went there and some men working on a tractor told me that the Senator had died and his widow, the English woman, was living in Siena.'

Evan E. Murdock, Colonel, Corps of Engineers, US Army (Ret).

Colonel, then Major Murdock, was later injured just about a mile from Monterosi when a bright orange flame hit the vehicle ahead, probably a mine or gunshot – beginning his nineteen months in hospital.

The US 1st Armored and 34th Infantry Divisions encountered serious difficulties in the mountainous area near Grosseto and Massa. Apart from the usual demolitions, mines and booby traps, the Germans frequently set up road blocks: Mark VI tanks waited with their 88-millimetre guns aimed at a bend, ready to annihilate anything in sight. Due to the ruggedness of the terrain, such obstacles could not be by-passed by wheeled and tracked vehicles.

The advance came to a halt in front of the ancient Etruscan fortress town of Volterra where the 88th and the 91st Divisions intervened. The former assaulted the town and proceeded northwards in two columns. The left one, spearheaded by the 351st Infantry Regiment met German strongholds at Laiatico and on Hills 184 and 188, which passed into history under the name of 'Bloody Ridge'. The 3rd Battalion of the 351st was awarded the Distinguished Unit Citation for its outstanding performance at Laiatico.

Reconnaissance patrols from the 88th Division reached the Arno on 19 July, and the whole division occupied the south bank of the river from San Romano to San Miniato.

The 34th Division captured the important port of Leghorn on 19 July. The French Corps was at Certaldo, and the 8th Indian Division in the outskirts of Empoli.

On 1 July, the Germans broadcast to the world that Florence was an open city so that its irreplaceable art treasures could be preserved. None the less, they were reluctant to abandon it and kept several divisions spread to cover its southern approaches. San Casciano fell on 27 July, then Giogoli, Impruneta and Incisa and other suburban villages. By this stage, the Germans had retreated to the north side of the Arno and blew up five of the six bridges over the river, except the Ponte Vecchio, although they demolished the houses at both ends of it to create road impediments. However, by 5 August, the whole southern bank of the Arno had been occupied by the Allied forces, with the exception of Montelupo and some areas east of the city.

## Adriatic Sector

By the end of June, after the battle for Lake Trasimeno, the Germans had begun retreating on the whole Italian front. They

**Plate XXVII**
The badges of the 10th Indian Division and of some British armoured formations are illustrated on this plate.

The 97th Field Regiment, RA, in the 10th Indian Division, was formed by the West and East Kent Yeomanry. All ranks wore the White Horse of Kent on the left sleeve as the horse was the emblem of both former regiments.

The 1st Armoured Division wore two formation signs at different periods; undoubtedly, also the first, 'North African' pattern, was used in Italy. The 9th Queen's Royal Lancers wore a special regimental flash because yellow and red were the colours of the Royal Armoured Corps and also the regimental colours of the 9th Lancers.

The 7th Armoured Brigade and the 21st and 25th Tank Brigades arrived in Italy in April-May 1944. They were formed by tank regiments and by the North Irish Horse, the latter in the 25th Brigade until December and then in the 21st Tank Brigade which on 11 June 1945 was redesignated 21st Armoured Brigade. In January 1945, the 25th Tank Brigade became an armoured assault brigade.

The Royal Wiltshire and the Warwickshire Yeomanry of the 9th Brigade were replaced in October 1944 by the 4th and by the 7th Hussars.

Lastly, on the bottom row is the cap badge of the 14th/20th King's Hussars, in Allied Armies reserve and the formation sign of the 1st Armoured Replacement Group, Central Mediterranean Force.

They came and went on to liberate others. After the celebrations, the task began of clearing the wreckage of a five-year war and building the future. *Polish Institute and Sikorski Museum Collection*

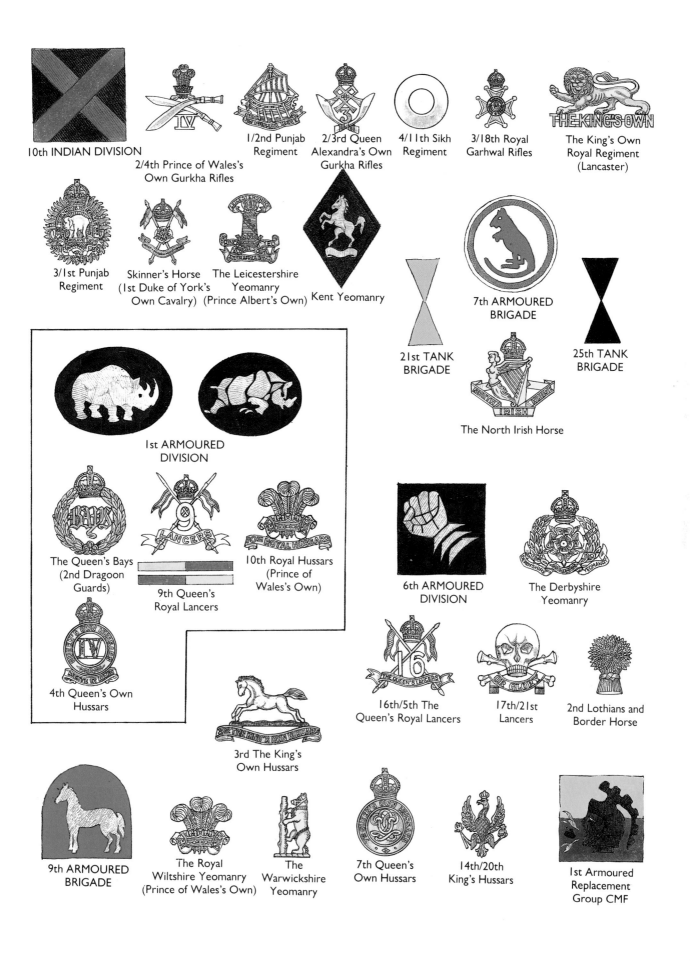

10th INDIAN DIVISION

2/4th Prince of Wales's
Own Gurkha Rifles

1/2nd Punjab
Regiment

2/3rd Queen
Alexandra's Own
Gurkha Rifles

4/11th Sikh
Regiment

3/18th Royal
Garhwal Rifles

The King's Own
Royal Regiment
(Lancaster)

3/1st Punjab
Regiment

Skinner's Horse
(1st Duke of York's
Own Cavalry)

The Leicestershire
Yeomanry
(Prince Albert's Own)

Kent Yeomanry

7th ARMOURED
BRIGADE

21st TANK
BRIGADE

25th TANK
BRIGADE

The North Irish Horse

1st ARMOURED
DIVISION

The Queen's Bays
(2nd Dragoon
Guards)

9th Queen's
Royal Lancers

10th Royal Hussars
(Prince of
Wales's Own)

6th ARMOURED
DIVISION

The Derbyshire
Yeomanry

4th Queen's Own
Hussars

16th/5th The
Queen's Royal Lancers

17th/21st
Lancers

2nd Lothians and
Border Horse

3rd The King's
Own Hussars

9th ARMOURED
BRIGADE

The Royal
Wiltshire Yeomanry
(Prince of Wales's Own)

The
Warwickshire
Yeomanry

7th Queen's
Own Hussars

14th/20th
King's Hussars

1st Armoured
Replacement
Group CMF

abandoned their defences on the River Chienti, leaving it to the 2nd Polish Corps Macerata and Recanati.

The possession of the port of Ancona was particularly important to the Allies, so the Germans were reluctant to surrender it. The battle began on 8 July, when Italians of the 'Nembo' Division attacked Filottrano. Three hundred were killed on the first day. Subsequently, the Polish and the Italian Corps crossed the Musone river, slowly pushing back the German defences. Field Marshal Kesselring arrived at Ancona on 16 July with the aim of boosting the morale of his troops but the town fell two days later. Leghorn, on the Tyrrhenian side, was captured on the same day. Both Ancona and Leghorn harbours had been demolished and their waterways blocked with sunken vessels. The battle for Ancona cost the Germans two divisions, the 71st and the 278th. Both were later partially reconstructed.

On 19 July, the Poles crossed the Esimo, one of the many rivers in that sector, and the Italians took Jesi. Moreover, due to strong German opposition near Ostra, another ten days went by before they could reach the next river, the Misa, where another battle developed for the town of Senigallia. On 11 August, the Cesano was crossed; the Italians on the left flank took Pergola on 19 August. Four days later, the Polish Corps was across the Metauro river.

The Italian Liberation Corps was put under the command of 5th Corps on 25 August in support of the 4th Indian Division aiming for Urbino and Urbania south of the Foglia river. On its northern bank were the first outposts of the 'Gothic' Line.

Bologna, May 1945. A warrant officer of the 3rd Carpathian Division holding the drum major's mace, which is the traditional 'ciupaga', the Polish highlanders axe-head stick. In the background is the HQ of the Allied Military Government. *Polish Institute and Sikorski Museum Collection*

# 6 The 'Gothic' Line

From 1943, the German Headquarters had realised the potential of the Appennines north of Tuscany and the Marche as a natural barrier for the defence of Southern Europe and began constructing fortifications among the mountains and valleys. This defensive line was initially called 'Green' Line. It started at Marina di Carrara, barring the way to the region of Liguria, and crossed the mountains, where steel and concrete fortifications guarded roads and passes, down to the Foglia river in the Adriatic sector.

More than a quarter of a million people, mainly conscripted Italians, were reported to have worked on these constructions. The fortifications included tunnels and underground shelters of all sizes, about five hundred emplacements for guns and mortars and over two thousand for machine guns. Secondary lines of defence were built also to give depth to the line as a whole.

If the central sector of the 'Gothic' Line were to hold, any break-through on its sides could be dangerous to the assailant army as it could be attacked on its flank. The weakest part of the line was its eastern end but only a massive army could venture into the Po valley and the Allies did not possess enough strength for this task.

The American contingent destined for the landing in the south of France – Operation ANVIL, now redesignated DRAGOON – had been withdrawn already, as the landing was scheduled for 15 August. The last to leave the front line was the French Expeditionary Force. The loss of this corps, although expected, was a serious blow to the Allied Armies in Italy as it was formed by troops specialised in mountain warfare who had proven their value throughout the previous campaign. An acute lack of infantry was felt at this stage as infantry in particular were needed to assault the 'Gothic' Line.

## THE GERMANS

The German Army suffered immense losses from Salerno onwards, but now, deployed on a powerful defensive line, it was a force to reckon with – still larger than the Allied Armies in Italy gauged by the number of divisions. Four Italian divisions were stationed in the north-west of Italy and innumerable fascist irregular formations were guarding the German lines of communications.

The 14th and the 10th Army were deployed on the 'Gothic' Line from west to east, and were composed of the units shown as follows:

MOUNTAIN

10th MOUNTAIN DIVISION

PENINSULA BASE SECTION

Combat Infantryman

Expert Infantryman

88th BLUE DEVIL DIV

456th ITALY ENGRS

88th 337-FA.BN. ITALY DIV

ITALY 88TH BLUE DEVIL DIV

TRUST

TRIESTE US TROOPS

Divisional Headquarters

88th 'BLUE DEVIL' INFANTRY DIVISION IN ITALY

349th, 350th and 351st Infantry Regiments

337th, 338th, 339th and 931st Field Artillery Battalions

132nd Infantry Regiment

Combat Leader 349th Infantry Regiment

34th MP Company

34th Signal Company

313th Engineers Battalion

313th Medical Battalion

88th Signal Company

88th MP Company

752nd Tank Battalion

760th Tank Battalion

**Plate XXVIII**
By the spring of 1945 the war had destroyed everything in its path. Industry and commerce hardly existed, especially in the north. The Italians were willing to trade with the Allies but there was little to offer.

The Italians noticed the colourful shoulder titles of the British troops and the fact that the Americans did not wear any, so they made them, mainly for the 88th Division, stationed in the north-east.

The clover leaf was of blue cloth, with embroidered edging in gold, silver or red thread for the artillery, and yellow for reconnaissance. Scrolls of varying sizes displaying the unit's title matched the clover leaf. These were unofficial badges that the GIs purchased in civilian shops.

However, when a special shoulder sleeve insignia was adopted in 1947 for the US Army contingent in the Free Territory of Trieste, it was a clover leaf below a scroll, obviously inspired by the unofficial badges made for the 88th Division.

When the Allies reached the 'Gothic' Line, some units had metal and enamel distinctive insignia made by local manufacturers in Florence. The 88th Division had badges made in Florence by Ricci. Later, when the 349th Infantry Regiment ran out of them, Lieutenant Peter V. Heinen approached the firm A. E. Lorioli, in Milan, and more were produced.

The South Africans had cap badges of the 'Q' Services Corps made in Florence and several British units purchased badges in Italy. The Shropshire Yeomanry, for example, ordered a number of cap badges, the King's Regiment had shoulder titles embroidered there, and the North Staffords their regimental flash.

**Polish Map of Central Italy** (overleaf)
A Polish map of Central Italy which shows the Allied Forces approaching the 'Gothic' Line on 23 July 1944. The Polish abbreviations of the titles of the units on the field are not difficult to understand: 'Piech' stands for Infantry, 'Strz' for Rifles, 'Panc' for Armoured, 'Górska' for Mountain and 'Spad' stands for Parachute. *Polish Institute and Sikorski Museum*

**14th Army**
14th Corps
  16th SS Panzer-Grenadier Division
  65th Infantry Division
  26th Panzer Division
1st Parachute Corps
  4th Parachute Division
  362nd Infantry Division
  356th Infantry Division
Reserve
  20th *Luftwaffe* Field Division
  29th Panzer-Grenadier Division

**10th Army**
51st Mountain Corps
  715th Infantry Division
  334th Infantry Division
  305th Infantry Division
  44th Infantry Division
  114th Mountain Division
76th Panzer Corps
  5th Mountain Division
  71st Infantry Division
  278th Infantry Division
Reserve
  1st Parachute Division
  162nd (Turcoman) Infantry Division
General Reserve
  98th Infantry Division

## THE ADVANCE TO THE 'GOTHIC' LINE

On 11 August, the Germans withdrew from Florence, taking with them, for safe keeping, part of the art treasures, all the medical equipment that they could find in the city and the copper cables from the tram lines. AMG officials went across the Arno ahead of the troops to reconnoitre the situation.

On the western sector, the Americans had occupied all the territory south of the Arno by 23 July and started to cross the river. The northern part of Pisa was taken by 2 September, Lucca on the 6th and Prato on the 10th. The South Africans entered Pistoia on the same day and Viareggio was occupied on 16 September.

### Allied Reorganisation
Several rearrangements and reorganisations took place in the Allied lines pending an assault on the 'Gothic' Line. The US 5th Army took over the area from the Tyrrhenean coast to Florence, with the US 4th Corps on the left, the US 2nd Corps in the centre and the British 13th Corps on its right. The latter was formed by the British 6th and the South African 6th Armoured Divisions, the 1st British and the 8th Indian Infantry Divisions. The 10th Corps was on the right flank of the 13th. The 5th Corps was on the eastern side of the Appennines with the 2nd Polish Corps and the 1st Canadian Corps. This hurried, major rearrangement of formations was perfectly executed, the idea being to break the 'Gothic' Line before the Germans had time to reorganise their troops on it, and before winter.

The three British corps in the Adriatic sector were confronted by the reconstructed 71st and 278th Infantry Divisions which had been badly mauled at Ancona, by the 1st Parachute Division and by the 5th Mountain Division.

Operation OLIVE, the break-through on the Adriatic sector, consisted of assaulting the preliminary German defences on the Foglia river without artillery preparation. The 2nd Polish Corps on the right flank would open the offensive, followed by the 1st

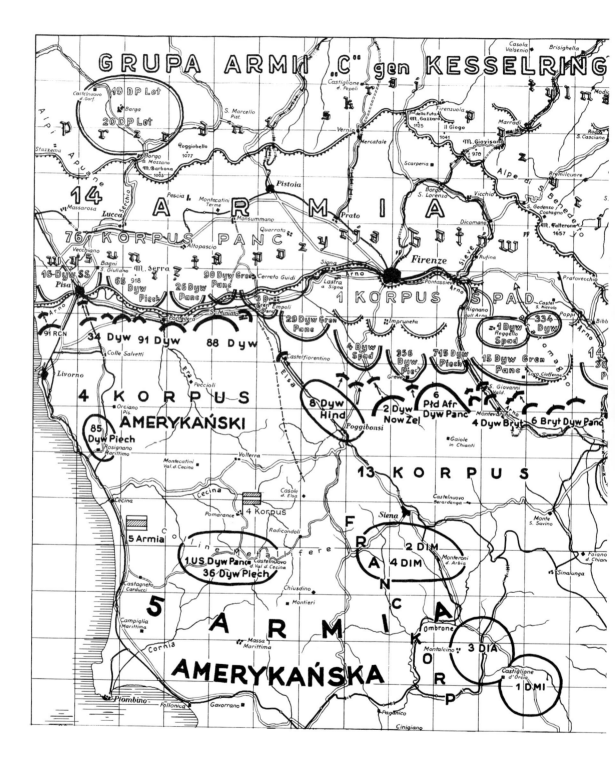

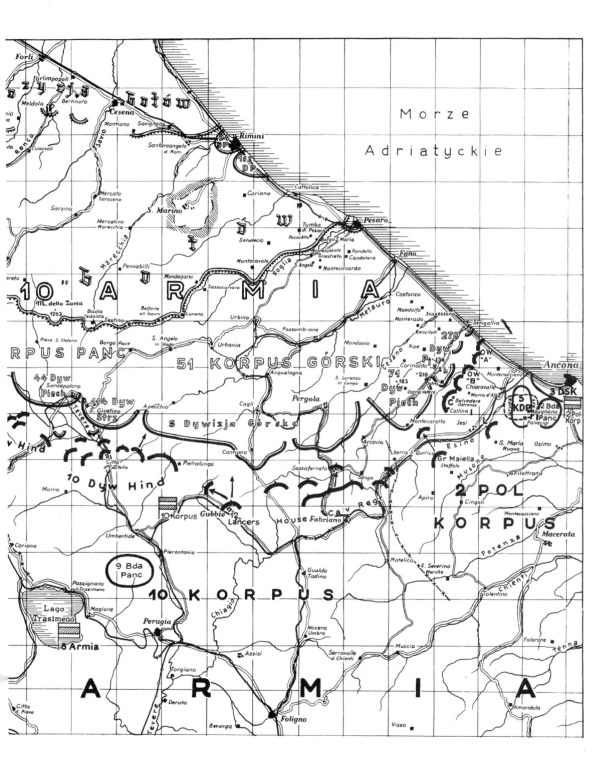

Forlì
Forlimpopoli
Meldola
Bertinoro
Cesena
Montiano
Savignano
Cusercoli
Santarcangelo
d. Rom.
Rimini
Mercato
Saraceno
S. Marino
Coriano
Cattolica
Sarzina
Mercatino
Marecchia
Saludecio
Pennabilli
Mondagano
Montecavalo
S. Angelo
Sassocorvaro
Belforte
all'Isauro
M. della Zucca
1263
Badia
Tedalda
Sestino
Lunano
Urbino
Fossombrone
Pieve S. Stefano
S. Angelo
in Vado
Urbania
Borgo Pace

Morze
Adriatyckie

Tomba
di Pesaro
Borgo S. Maria
Pozzo Alto
Montelabbate
Ginestreto
Rondello
Candelara
Montecchio
Fano

Costanzo
Mondolfo
Monterado
Scapezzano
Senigallia
Rancitelli
278
Dyw
P.
136
Ripe
Ancona
Corinaldo
71
210
Montemarciano
183
Dyw
Ostra Vetere
OW "B"
Chiaravalle
Piech
Ostra
Belvedere
Ostrense
Marro d'Alba
Collina
Montecarotto
Iesi
Montecarotto
Esino
S. Maria
Nuova
Osimo
Gr Maiella
Staffolo
Filottrano

Pesaro

OW "A"

3 DSK
5 KDP
2 Bda
Panc
2 Pol
Korp

RPUS PANC
44 Dyw
Piech
Sansepolcro
114 Dyw
S. Giustino
Strz
Apecchio
Cagli
Pergola
Acqualagna
S. Lorenzo
in Campo

51 KORPUS GÓRSKI

5 Dywizja Górska

Apiro
Cingoli
Montecassiano
Macerata

v Hind
Città
d'Castello
Pietralunga
Sassoferrato
Genga
Arcevia
Serra S'Quirico

2 POL
KORPUS

10 Dyw Hind
Morra
10 Korpus
Gubbio
12
Lancers
Cav Reg
House Fabriano
Matelica
S. Severino
Marche

Umbertide
Pierantonio

9 Bda
Panc

10 KORPUS

Coriona
Passignano
sul Trasimeno
Gualdo
Tadino
Potenza
Tolentino

Lago
Trasimeno
Magione
Chiagio
Perugia
Nocera
Umbra
Muccia
Serravalle
d. Chienti
Falerone
Tenna
Amandola

8 Armia
Torgiano
Assisi

Città
d. Pieve
Deruta
Bevanga
Foligno
Visso

A R M I A

125

Canadian Corps, designated to take over. The 5th Corps, the largest corps formation on the battlefield, was to operate on the hilly left flank of the Adriatic sector, bearing north-east towards Bologna after the break-through. When, after a few days, the Germans had moved their reserves to that sector, the 5th Army would launch its offensive in the central sector. The Germans would rearrange their reserves to face the new threat. At this stage, 8th Army could assault their last defensive lines.

To make these plans possible, the British 46th and 56th Divisions returned from the Middle East and one Greek Brigade joined the 8th Army before the offensive. The British armoured divisions were formed by one armoured and one infantry brigade leaving some independent armoured brigades free to support infantry formations as the necessity arose.

The US 1st Armored Division was reorganised: its two armored regiments were reformed into three tank battalions, designated the 1st, 4th and 13th; the infantry regiment was split into three separate battalions, namely the 6th, 11th and 14th; and minor changes affected the rest of the other divisional units. In this manner the division now could operate in three separate combat commands.

The 6th South African Armoured Division was transferred to US 4th Corps. Its place in the 13th British Corps was taken by the 1st Canadian Armoured Brigade.

A new American division, the 92nd, reinforced the US 5th Army, in 4th Corps. Task Force 45 and the Brazilian Expeditionary Force also reinforced the US 5th Army.

The Allied Armies were deployed as tabulated here, from east to west:

A private of the 14th Engineers Company, identified by the badge he wears on his beret. The black panther was the emblem of the 14th 'Wielkopolska' Armoured Brigade and '41' is his unit's vehicle service number. *Polish Institute and Sikorski Museum Collection*

**British 8th Army**
2nd Polish Corps (in reserve after the
    initial attack)
  3rd 'Karpathian' Rifle Division
  5th 'Kresowa' Infantry Division
  2nd Armoured Brigade
1st Canadian Corps
  1st Canadian Infantry Division
  2nd New Zealand Division
  5th Canadian Armoured Division
  21st Tank Brigade
  3rd Greek Mountain Brigade
5th Corps
  4th Infantry Division
  4th Indian Division
  46th (North Midland) Infantry
    Division
  56th (London) Division
  1st Armoured Division
  7th Armoured Brigade
  25th Tank Brigade
10th Corps
  10th Indian Division
  9th Armoured Brigade

**US 5th Army**
13th British Corps
  1st Infantry Division
  8th Indian Division
  6th Armoured Division
  1st Canadian Armoured Brigade
2nd Corps
  34th Infantry Division 'Red Bull'
  85th Infantry Division 'Custer'
  88th Infantry Division 'Blue Devil'
  91st Infantry Division 'Powder River'
  Task Force 45
4th Corps
  6th South African Armoured Division
  92nd Infantry Division 'Buffalo'
  Combat Team 442

Reserve
  1st Armored Division
  Brazilian Expeditionary Force

### 92nd Infantry Division 'Buffalo'

The 92nd was one of two divisions raised during World War Two formed mainly by negroes, thence the nickname as the American Indians used to call negroes 'buffaloes' because of their thick curly hair. Both divisions already existed as an experiment during World War One and saw action in France.

The 92nd Division was activated at Fort McClellan, Alabama, on 15 October 1942, and moved to Fort Huachuca, Arizona, in April 1943. It participated in the Louisiana manoeuvres from 7 February to 3 April 1944.

In June 1944, the division was transferred to North Africa, and from there to Italy. By mid-August, it had taken up positions on the Arno river in a defensive role.

**92nd Infantry Division 'Buffalo'**

| | |
|---|---|
| 365th, 370th and 371st Infantry Regiments | 317th Medical Battalion |
| 597th, 598th, 599th and 600th Field Artillery Battalions | 92nd Signal Company |
| 317th Engineers Battalion | 792nd Ordnance Company |
| | 92nd Quartermaster Company |
| | 92nd Reconnaissance Troop |

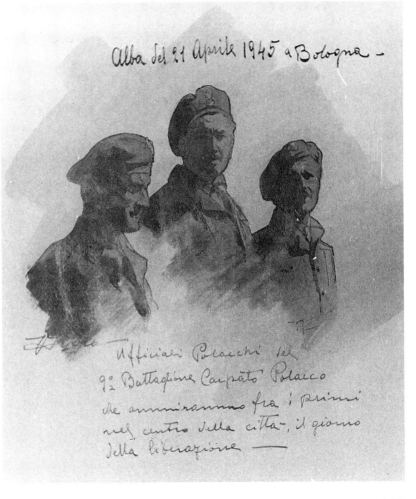

Dawn on 11 April 1945 at Bologna. A sketch of three Polish officers of the 9th Carpathian Battalion, who were among the first to arrive in the city centre on the day of the Liberation. *Polish Institute and Sikorski Museum Collection*

*Task Force 45*

This formation was formed by three groups each of regiment strength. It was used in a defensive role.

*Brazilian Expeditionary Force*

Brazil declared war on Germany and Italy on 22 August 1942 and broke off diplomatic relations with Japan. Its initial contribution to the Allied cause was an intensive campaign against U-boats in the South Atlantic.

In January 1943, at a meeting in Natal between President Roosevelt and the Brazilian President Vargas, it was decided that Brazilian troops should join the Allied armies. Plans were made for equipping and training a force of 300,000 for overseas service. At the beginning of December 1943, a Brazilian Military Mission arrived in North Africa. Led by General Joao B. Mascarenhas de Moreas, the mission examined the possibilities of Brazilian co-operation in the Mediterranean Theatre of Operations.

On 16 July 1944, the 1st Expeditionary Infantry Division began disembarking at Naples. It arrived in five contingents, the third in October, the rest later, but Brazilian troops were already on the front line in September. Redesignated the Brazilian Expeditionary Force, it formed part of the 5th US Army. Its troops were armed, dressed and equipped by the Americans.

**Força Expedicionaria Brasileira**

Infantry
  1st Infantry Regiment (Sampaio Regiment)
  6th Infantry Regiment (Ipiranga Regiment)
  11th Infantry Regiment (Tiradented Regiment)
Artillery
  1st Regiment (three groups)
  2nd Regiment (one group)

Engineers
  9th Engineer Battalion
Medical
  1st Battalion
Others
  Signal, Maintenance, Administrative Companies
  Reconnaissance Squadron
  Police Platoon
  Divisional Band

## THE ASSAULT ON THE 'GOTHIC' LINE

### 8th Army

Operation OLIVE began from the Metauro river on the night of 25/26 August 1944, with the Canadians and the 46th Division spearheading the advance. By 31 August the first German defences on the 'Green' Line, beyond the Foglia river, had been passed. Cattolica was taken and the Conca river was crossed by the Canadians on 3 September. The German 26th Panzer, the 29th Panzer-Grenadier and the 98th Infantry Division intervened in the battle, followed by the 162nd (Turcoman) Division.

The 1st Armoured Division had a slow start and arrived in action at Coriano where its infantry captured Passano and San Savino. Riccione fell, the Marano river was crossed, and the 4th Indian Division occupied San Marino.

The battle on approaching Rimini was one of the most bitter of

The liberation of Bologna: the Italian generals Cevica and Utili, and in the centre, the city's mayor, Dozza. The Polish general in the background is in fact the Liberator, rather bored by the endless speeches. Cevica wears the old grey-green uniform with silver embroidered cap badge. Utili wears British battledress and grey-green forage cap with his general's badge in black thread. *Polish Institute and Sikorski Museum Collection*

the campaign, with hand-to-hand fighting in every village. The Canadians captured San Lorenzo on 20 September and Rimini at last fell on 21 September.

## 5th Army

The 'Gothic' Line had been breached. Meanwhile, in the central sector, the Allied troops continued to advance slowly, closing up to the main German defences. On 12 September, their offensive began. The US 2nd Corps, 34th Division was deployed in a diversionary role against the Futa pass, and the corps' 91st Division moved towards the Giogo Pass; both passes are north of Florence on the routes to Bologna. The British 13th Corps began advancing towards Faenza and Forlì.

As the German 356th Division had been moved to the Adriatic sector, the 1st Parachute Corps did not have enough strength to contain the US 2nd Corps, which was massively supported by the Allied air force. The 91st and 85th Divisions captured the Giogo pass on 18 September, and the Futa fell also.

On their right flank, 13th Corps managed to break through the main German defences by 15 September. The 1st Division secured the Casaglia pass and reached Palazzuolo on 24 September and the 6th Armoured Division captured San Benedetto in Alpe.

The Americans immediately pushed forward four 2nd Corps' divisions, the 34th, the 85th and the 91st towards Bologna, and the 88th Division on the road to Imola. The latter arrived at Castel del Rio, almost in the Po valley, by 25 September. Entrenched on Mount Battaglia, it repulsed several German counter-attacks until relieved by 13th Corps troops.

By the end of September, half of the 'Gothic' Line, from Florence to the Adriatic, had been crushed. General Clark ordered another attack to commence on 1 October, deploying the whole 2nd Corps reinforced by the British 78th Division, fresh from Egypt, and the 6th South African Armoured Division on the left flank. The Germans, aware of impending disaster, sent all available resources and a vicious battle began.

Mount Grande was captured by troops of the 349th Regiment of the 88th Division on 19 October but Vedriano, a village north-east of Mount Grande could not be taken, although orders continued to arrive to take it. The 88th Division was at a distance of less than 9,000 yards from Highway 9, whose capture could have ended the war in Italy.

Apart from fierce German resistance, the weather had been deteriorating constantly, bringing driving rain and sleet to the entire front. The troops were bogged down in mud. The offensive was called off.

## 8th Army

The advance continued on the Adriatic sector. The Savio and the Ronco rivers were crossed at the end of October. The 2nd Polish Corps, returning to the battlefield after a short period of rest, occupied Predappio, the birthplace of Mussolini, and Castrocaro, on 27 October. On the Poles' right flank, 5th Corps took Forlì on 9 November. Subsequently, the Poles by-passed Faenza, crossed the Lamone, captured the town of Brisighella and reached the Senio river. Ravenna fell on 4 December and Faenza on 16 December 1944.

All operations ceased at the end of December.

## Redeployments

At the end of November 1944, Mark W. Clark was promoted to the command of the Allied Armies in Italy in place of Alexander; Alexander replaced General Sir H. Maitland Wilson in command of the Mediterranean theatre. Lt General Sir Richard L. McCreery became the commander of the 8th Army and Maj. General Lucian K. Truscott was appointed to command the US 5th Army. In December 1944, the Allied Armies in Italy were redesignated 15th Army Group, their original title in Sicily.

At the beginning of March 1945, Field Marshal Kesselring, upon being appointed Commander-in-Chief West, was replaced in Italy by General von Vietinghoff. Earlier, Obergruppenführer Karl Wolff, head of the security SS in Italy, sent emissaries to the American Embassy in Zurich to commence negotiations for the surrender of the German forces in Italy. Inevitably, General von Vietighoff became involved in this diplomacy. It had become clear, at last, to the Germans that they had lost the war; or, at least, it was clear to the senior officers.

## Allied Air Forces

The *Luftwaffe* was withdrawn from Italy. The task of air defence was left to the air force of the Italian Social Republic, keen on the task, fairly well equipped, but with little or no fuel.

The Allied air forces had complete air supremacy. Apart from supporting their ground forces, they monitored every movement on land, day and night, in the whole territory of northern Italy.

Maj. General Livesay awards the Silver Star to 1st Lieutenant John Gualtney in May 1945, near Gorizia. *R. Livengood Collection*

Anything that moved in daylight on the roads was bombed or machine-gunned, according to size. Aircraft flew during the night looking for lights or any sign of life on the ground.

Every airfield and military target, railway station and junction, and every bridge was bombed, rebuilt and destroyed again. The Americans blasted towns and cities during the day and the British during the night. Massive formations of aircraft flew over northern Italy on their way to Austria and Bavaria, and back, too many to be challenged.

The Headquarters of the Mediterranean Allied Tactical Air Force had moved to Siena and those of the Desert Air Force were at Cattolica. There were also headquarters of the Mediterranean Allied Coastal Air Force at Caserta and of the Balkan Air Force at Bari. The latter flew over Yugoslavia, mainly to supply Tito's Liberation Army which was the principal task of the newly formed Royal Italian Air Force.

Two Yugoslav and three Royal Hellenic Air Force fighter squadrons were in Italy in December 1944. The Poles had three squadrons: No 301 (Special Duty) Squadron with Halifaxes and Liberators at Brindisi; No 318 Squadron with Spitfires at Rimini; and No 663 Squadron with AOP Austers at Eboli. The 'Ardennes' Squadron of the French Air Force was still in Italy. The South Africans had the largest contingent among the Commonwealth air forces, with nineteen squadrons, including two flying Liberators. The Allied air forces had grown to gigantic proportions.

## THE AMG AND THE ITALIANS

In February 1944, the seat of the Italian Government and the headquarters of the Allied Control Commission were transferred from Brindisi to Salerno. As it was impossible to find quarters for all the ministries and departments in the new 'capital', some went to Naples, while others had to remain at Brindisi. Finally, on 15 July 1944 both organisations moved to Rome. After the liberation, Rome had become an AMG region for a month and was then returned to Italian administration, together with Region III and IV. The city of Naples remained under Allied administration, and later also Ancona and Leghorn and some minor ports were used as supply bases.

### Italian Governments

Marshal Badoglio attempted but failed to form a composite government representing all the anti-fascist parties which were grouped in the National Liberation Committee (CLN) set up in Naples. None of these parties wanted to collaborate with either the King or the marshal as both of them had prospered under Mussolini's regime.

In November 1943, Badoglio had formed a cabinet of 'experts' but at the end of January 1944, the six parties forming the CLN had held a congress at Bari in which a motion was raised asking for the abdication of King Victor Emmanuel III. Confronted with this situation, the King had announced his decision to retire into private life and to appoint his son Umberto, Prince of Piedmont, as Lieutenant of the Realm. At the beginning of May, Marshal Badoglio had formed a new government which included representatives of the CLN. On the liberation of Rome on 4 July, the King resigned and Prince Umberto became Lieutenant of the Realm. In accordance with constitutional custom, a new government was formed, led by Ivanoe Bonomi, in place of Badoglio.

Legal complications arose after the formation of the Italian Social Republic in northern Italy. As a result, all the civil servants in Allied-occupied territory formerly belonging to the Italian Social Republic were considered traitors by the Italian administration in the south, but not enough replacements were available there.

## The Resistance

The CLN also acted as an underground organisation in the German-occupied territory of the Republic and elected among its members the officials of the new civil administrations of the liberated territories. Nonetheless, the choice of the CLN often did not suit the AMG officials.

The resistance movement grew stronger politically and militarily, especially in the north, where the National Liberation Committee for Northern Italy (CLNAI) was formed, which started to issue its own orders, often countermanding those from the main committee, in Rome. The northerners felt that they alone were suffering the horrors of war to its bitter end and were not prepared to be imposed upon by pen-pushers under the protection of the liberators.

The Allied troops met the first 'patriots' in Naples and later on the Appennines. One partisan unit, the 'Brigata Maiella' operated with the Polish 2nd Corps on the Adriatic sector, but when they reached Tuscany and the 'Gothic' Line they met highly-politicised *resistants*, usually communists, in brigades grouped into divisions.

The task of the AMG was to maintain public order in the occupied territories just behind the front line on behalf of the Italian administration. The Military Police dealt with problems connected with military personnel and the Civil Police formed by the Carabinieri Reali dealt with civilian affairs. Nonetheless, the AMG became involved in endless controversies as partisans in the newly-occupied areas set their own rules of law and objected to surrendering their arms to the Carabinieri. The Carabinieri followed the Allies' advance under AMG control; for instance, three hundred and sixty were sent into Florence immediately after its liberation. Officials from the CLN were attached to AMG commands with the task of sorting out problems connected with the Resistance.

The task of the Resistance lay in German-occupied territory. Once an area was liberated by the Allies, the local partisan formations had to be disbanded but many men came from the north, or from abroad, and therefore they had to be temporarily resettled in camps, at Florence, Pescia, Ravenna, Forlì and later at Faenza.

In December 1944, the 8th Army enrolled one thousand five hundred partisans as reconnaissance troops. In February 1945, five partisan detachments were attached to Italian combat groups in the same role.

The Italian Government, by now in full control of half of the peninsula, did not want to be subordinated to the Allies. The Allied Control Commission had to be redesignated Allied Commission.

## THE GERMANS

During the winter of 1944–45, the *Wehrmacht* was holding hopeless positions which could not be held for long in the event of an Allied offensive. An Allied offensive was inevitable. The Germans gathered all available troops. By mid-October 1944, the Italian 'Monterosa' Mountain Division with two battalions from the 'San Marco' were placed on the 'Gothic' Line to confront the Brazilian Expeditionary Force. However, German units, in turn, had to be sent to the western Alps to reinforce the Italian formations guarding the French-Italian border.

The German's lines of communication were continuously sabotaged by the partisans and bombed and machine-gunned by the Allied air forces. Although new fortified lines were in the process of being built on the Po, Adige and farther east on the Isonzo river, it was doubtful that the Germans, once in retreat in the exposed Po valley, could ever reach them.

Civil war was raging between fascist units and the partisans, and the fascists seemed unable to control the situation. Several

Relaxing . . . Lieutenants Larson, Dale N. Boyd and John J. Schreibeis, of the 363rd Infantry Regiment, 91st Division, in Milan, July 1945. *R. Livengood Collection*

*rastrellamenti* ('raking' operations) took place during the winter. Troops would surround a vast area and advance towards its centre checking every building, every wood and every possible hiding place. Often battles developed and, although the hunted usually managed to slip away, both sides suffered severe casualties, quite apart from the distress inflicted on the population caught between the contestants.

---

### Rastrellamento

'The mention of this word would immediately revive haunting memories to those who experienced it. They were usually farmers or inhabitants of rural villages, the ideal ground for active Resistance units.

'Due to lack of food supplies the fascist administration, under the vigilance of the Germans, registered in detail the stock of every farm as all products were stockpiled and redistributed by the Germans. The farmers sold privately on the black market what they managed to hide but, at the same time, they were compelled to feed the partisans, who lived in the woods nearby.

'The Germans, supported by Italian troops, especially by local Black Brigades and other irregular fascist units, mounted massive *rastrellamenti* in order to break up the Resistance. Entire divisions with tanks raked through large areas: every wood, every house, every room of each house and every ditch were searched for partisans. Often fierce battles developed as partisans could not surrender. If caught one was interrogated and then shot or hanged.

'Any proof or the mere suspicion of abetting the *Banditen* was severely punished: the house owners could pack one suitcase per head and then the house was burned with flame-throwers.

'This was the least that could happen. In certain cases the village population was rounded up in the church which was blown up and the entire village was set to flames.

'In those days one could not complain to the police about it, or write to the local newspaper!'

G. Rosignoli.

---

In December 1944, the Germans and Italians prepared an offensive, their last, in the Serchio river area. At the beginning of November 1944, the Brazilian Expeditionary Force had been relieved by the US 92nd 'Buffalo' Division of the 4th Corps in the area of the Serchio river. The German and Italian forces started their offensive, on the night of 25 December and pushed back the 'Buffaloes', opening a gap in 4th Corps front which was hastily secured by the 8th Indian Division, from 13th Corps.

The 'Monterosa' was replaced by the 1st Division 'Italia'. As the Germans switched formations, or combat groups of formations, from one area to another according to different circumstances, their order of battle changed constantly. The following is the last deployment of Army Group 'C' on the 'Gothic' Line from west to east.

316th Engineers, 91st Infantry Division, on furlough in Rome, in front of St Peter's Cathedral, trying to ignore the problems of an Italian. The men wear two different types of garrison cap. *R. Livengood Collection*

**Army Group 'C'**
**14th Army**
51st Corps
  148th Infantry Division
  232nd Infantry Division
  334th Infantry Division
  114th Mountain Division
  1st Bersaglieri Division 'Italia'
14th Panzer Corps
  94th Infantry Division
  8th Mountain Division

**10th Army**
1st Parachute Corps

1st Parachute Division
305th Infantry Division
278th Infantry Division
4th Parachute Division
98th Infantry Division
76th Corps
  44th Infantry Division
  362nd Infantry Division
  162nd Infantry Division
  29th Panzer-Grenadier Division

Reserve
  90th Panzer-Grenadier Division

## THE ALLIES

The 15th Army Group had to face several problems during the winter 1944–45. Many formations were in need of rest, reorganisation and re-training. At the same time, adequate forces had to be provided to prevent a civil war in Greece where the ELAS and EDES organisations were at war with each other.

The 2nd Parachute Brigade and the 23rd Armoured Brigade were sent to Greece in mid-October and the 4th Indian Division at the beginning of November, followed by the 4th and 46th Divisions. Of all these, only the 46th (North Midland) Infantry Division returned to Italy, on 11 March 1945.

The 1st Infantry Division went to Palestine at the end of January 1945. It remained there for the duration of the war.

On 10 January 1945, the 1st Armoured Division was disbanded and its 2nd Armoured Brigade was put under the command of the

1st Canadian Infantry Division. The 25th Tank Brigade was converted into an armoured assault brigade, specialising in assaulting and crossing rivers.

Worst of all, at the demand of the Canadian Government, the Combined Chiefs of Staff decided to reunite the two Canadian corps in the Netherlands. The 1st Canadian Corps left Italy in March 1945.

Several formations were reorganised: the 2nd New Zealand Division formed a third infantry brigade, the 9th, within its ranks, converting armoured units into infantry in two stages, in October 1944 and February 1945. A new unit the 28th Assault Squadron, was formed for crossing the Senio.

The 6th South African Armoured Division was reorganised on the same pattern as the 2nd New Zealand Division in order to create more infantry. On 13 January 1945, the South African 13th Brigade was formed from the following:

**13th South African Brigade**

Natal Mounted Rifles,
  formerly armoured reconnaissance
Royal Durban Light Infantry,
  formerly heavy weapons battalion
Imperial Light Horse-Kimberley
  Regiment, formerly an armoured
  regiment
1st Royal Natal Carbineers
Dukes – Scottish – Rand Light
  Infantry, consisting of very young
  soldiers, kept in reserve

These units were supported by:

15th Field Regiment, South African
  Artillery
5th Field Company, South African
  Engineer Corps
18th Motorised Brigade Signal
  Company

In April 1945, before the attack on Mount Sole, the brigades of the 6th South African Armoured Division were formed as shown in the following table.

**6th South African Armoured Division**

11th South African Armoured Brigade
  Pretoria Regiment
  Prince Alfred's Guards*
  Special Service Battalion*
  Imperial Light Horse/Kimberley
    Regiment
  1/135th Regimental Combat
    Team (US)
12th South African Motorised Brigade
  Royal Durban Light Infantry
  1st City Regiment/Cape Town
    Highlanders

  Witwatersrand Rifles/Regiment de
    la Rey
  4/13th Frontier Force Rifles (India)
  1st Squadron Prince Alfred's Guard
13th South African Motorised Brigade
  Royal Natal Carbineers
  Natal Mounted Rifles
  1st Squadron Special Service
    Battalion

*Not the complete unit.

The US 92nd 'Buffalo' Division was sent back to the front line in February 1945. Once again, its achievements were disappointing. Therefore, it was reorganised into one black regiment, one regiment formed by 'Nisei' (Japanese born in the USA), and one infantry regiment raised from anti-aircraft gunners. The division was moved to the left flank of 4th Corps before the spring offensive.

Another negro regiment was the 366th Infantry in Task Force 45. It was later joined by other units eliminated from the 92nd Division.

Although many divisions were waiting in the United States to be moved to the European Theatre of Operations, only one, the 10th Mountain Division, was sent to Italy. It was, as it turned out, one of the best.

### 10th Mountain Division

Organised in August 1918 as an infantry division but too late to be sent overseas, the 10th was disbanded in February 1919. On 15 July 1943, it was reactivated as 10th Division (L) and redesignated 10th Mountain Division on 6 November 1944. The division was formed at Camp Hale, Colorado. Later, moved to Camp Swift, Texas, it took part in the manoeuvres at the Hunter Liggett Military Reservation, training for mountain warfare. It contained a high percentage of expert skiiers, woodsmen and mountaineers and was provided with special mountain equipment.

The 87th regiment participated in the landing at Kiska.

In December 1944, the 10th Mountain Division was assigned to the Mediterranean Theatre of Operations.

**10th Mountain Division**

| | |
|---|---|
| 85th, 86th and 87th Mountain Infantry Regiments | 10th Medical Battalion |
| 604th, 605th and 616th (Pack Howitzer) Field Artillery Battalions | 110th Signal Company |
| | 710th Ordnance Company |
| | 10th Quartermaster Company |
| 126th Engineers Battalion | 10th Reconnaissance Troop |

### 25th Armoured Engineer Brigade, Royal Engineers

In January 1945, the 142nd Regiment, Royal Armoured Corps, was disbanded and the North Irish Horse was transferred to the 21st Tank Brigade to replace the 145th Regiment, RAC, which was also disbanded. The 25th Tank Brigade was redesignated 'B' Assault Brigade RAC/RE which in April was again redesignated 25th Armoured Engineer Brigade, RE. The objective of this conversion was to provide a formation specialised in assaulting and crossing rivers.

**25th Armoured Engineer Brigade, Royal Engineers**

51st Royal Tank Regiment
  'A' Armoured Regiment, RE
  'B' Armoured Regiment, RE
  'C' Armoured Park Squadron, RE

## The Italian Combat Groups

The raising of the combat groups in the autumn of 1944 marked the beginning of the expansion of the Italian Army as, after the

end of the conflict, the groups became divisions and replaced the Allied Forces in the defence of the nation.

Each combat group was manned by 432 officers and 8,578 other ranks, with 116 guns of various types, 170 mortars, 502 Bren guns and 1,277 vehicles. All ranks wore British uniforms.

*Gruppo di Combattimento 'Cremona'*
Originating from the 44th Infantry Division 'Cremona', which was stationed on the island of Corsica at the time of the armistice, this formation was moved to Italy where, on 25 September 1944, it was converted into a combat group. The 'Cremona' was deployed on the east side of the Alfonsine-Ravenna railway line, as part of the Canadian Corps.

**Gruppo di Combattimento 'Cremona'**
21° e 22° Reggimento Fanteria
7° Reggimento Artiglieria
Servizi

*Gruppo di Combattimento 'Legnano'*
At the beginning of September 1943, the 58th Infantry Division 'Legnano' was transferring from the south of France to the region of Puglie. Only part of the division arrived at its destination as other units were intercepted en route by the Germans.

The 67th Infantry Regiment, which was in the Puglie, fully

Fusiliers of the 9th Battalion of the 3rd Carpathian Division on 7 October 1945. They have just been awarded the medallion and certificate for the liberation of the city of Bologna, Italy, on 21 April 1945. On their berets they wear their special battalion badges. *Polish Institute and Sikorski Museum Collection*

138

equipped, became part of the 1st Motorised Group and the 68th, later, was part of the Italian Liberation Corps.

The 'Legnano' Group was constituted on 24 September 1944, with the units tabulated below. The group was initially attached to the 8th Army and later to the US 2nd Corps in the sector of the 91st Division.

**Gruppo di Combattimento**
**'Legnano'**

| | |
|---|---|
| 68° Reggimento Fanteria | Reggimento Fanteria Speciale |
|   I Battaglione 'Palermo' |   Battaglione Alpini 'Piemonte' |
|   II Battaglione 'Novara' |   Battaglione Alpini 'L'Aquila' |
|   Battaglione d'Assalto 'Col Moschin' |   Battaglione Bersaglieri 'Goito' |
|     (IX) | 11° Reggimento Artiglieria |
| | Servizi |

*Gruppo di Combattimento 'Friuli'*

The 20th Infantry Division 'Friuli' was with the 'Cremona' in Corsica. Back in Italy, it too became a combat group, on 10 September 1944. The Infantry* comprised one battalion of Grenadiers. The group was on the Adriatic sector, initially under the command of 5th Corps, later under the 2nd Polish Corps.

**Gruppo di Combattimento**
**'Friuli'**
87° e 88° Reggimento Fanteria*
35° Reggimento Artiglieria
Servizi

*Gruppo di Combattimento 'Folgore'*

The 'Folgore' originated from the 184th Parachute Division 'Nembo' which was in Sardinia at the time of the armistice and later, in Italy, became part of the Italian Liberation Corps.

The group was constituted on 24 September 1944 as a mixed unit, as its order of battle explains. The group was deployed in the area of Ascoli Piceno.

**Gruppo di Combattimento**
**'Folgore'**
Reggimento Paracadutisti 'Nembo'
Reggimento Marina 'San Marco'
  Battaglione 'Grado', 'Bafile' e
    'Caorle'
184° Reggimento Artiglieria 'Folgore'
Servizi

*Gruppo di Combattimento 'Mantova'*

The 104th Infantry Division 'Mantova' was in the region of Calabria at the time of the armistice. On 1 October 1943, its 113th Infantry Regiment was transferred to Naples where it became a labour unit of the US 5th Army. The division obtained the 185th Parachute Regiment as a replacement for this regiment and later the 76th Infantry Regiment. During February 1944, the 119th and the 120th Infantry Regiment were also assigned to the

'Mantova' which was split into two detachments, one of which remained in Calabria while the other was sent to the Puglie.

On 1 October 1944, the combat group was formed with the units tabulated below. The group was attached to the British 8th Army but did not participate in any operations.

**Gruppo di Combattimento**
**'Mantova'**
114° Reggimento Fanteria
76° Reggimento Fanteria
155° Reggimento Artiglieria
Servizi

*Gruppo di Combattimento 'Piceno'*

The 152nd Infantry Division 'Piceno' was stationed in the Puglie and was reorganised in February 1944. It became a combat group on 10 October 1944, with the original component units of the division, as tabulated below.

On 8 January 1945, the 'Piceno' Group was redesignated 'Division' again and became a recruits' training centre for the other combat groups, at Cesano, near Rome.

**Gruppo di Combattimento**
**'Piceno'**
235° e 236° Reggimento Fanteria
152° Reggimento Artiglieria
Servizi

*Squadrone da Ricognizione 'F'*

After the armistice, some units of the 185th Parachute Regiment joined the Canadians in the region of Calabria. On 15 November 1943, this contingent was put under the command of 13th Corps and, in December, was designated 1st Autonomous Special Detachment and redesignated 1st Reconnaissance Squadron 'F' in March 1944. It operated behind the enemy lines in the region of Emilia.

## The Jewish Brigade Group

From the outbreak of World War Two, the Zionists appealed to the British Government to agree to allow the formation of Jewish units. By the end of 1940, fifteen Jewish companies were in existence for the territorial defence of Palestine. These companies were grouped into three battalions which became the Jewish contingent of the Palestine Regiment, a British, Jewish and Arab unit formed in September 1942.

In the autumn of 1944, the formation of a Jewish brigade group was authorised by the British Government. It comprised about five thousand men and included the Jewish battalions formerly in the Palestine Regiment, an artillery regiment and all the ancillary units of a brigade group, under the command of Brigadier Ernest F. Benjamin.

The Jewish Brigade Group arrived in Italy in November 1944

The certificate for the liberation of the city of Bologna, awarded with a medallion to all ranks of the 3rd and 4th Company of the 9th Battalion, 3rd Carpathian Rifle Brigade and signed by the city's mayor, Guiseppe Dozza. *Polish Institute and Sikorski Museum Collection*

and trained on the Irpinian mountains until the end of February, when it was moved to the front line in the sector of Alfonsine, north-west of Ravenna. A few days later, the brigade group was transferred to the Senio river, which it crossed on 9 April. Later, it captured Mount Gabbio. After the end of the hostilities, the Jewish Brigade Group was stationed in an area between the regions of Alto Adige and Carnia.

### The Pack Transport Units

The mountainous terrain where the Germans established their main defensive lines called for the organisation of pack transport units to supply the Allied troops on the front line. The necessity of such units had already arisen in Sicily when the 78th Division, during its advance behind Mount Etna, requisitioned mules and donkeys which were driven by British soldiers and Italian civilians to re-supply the troops on the front line.

The same problem but on a larger scale was encountered on the 'Gustav' Line and pack transport units were formed officially, mainly from Cypriots and Italians, employed by the 8th Army and the 5th Army, respectively. These men had an unenviable and unrewarding task: hard work in dangerous conditions and in all kinds of weather, often carrying live ammunition and always under enemy fire, as the German gunners were keen on disrupting the Allied lines of communication.

The Cyprus Regiment, formed in April 1940, provided Pack and Mechanical Transport companies for the British 8th Army. The Italian units were formed by Italian soldiers, possibly experienced in dealing with mules, and by volunteers. They wore British uniforms dyed dark green and their own original head-dress, often the Alpine hat.

The efforts of at least one of these units should be mentioned, as an example. The 5° Reparto Salmerie 'Monte Cassino' (5th Pack Unit) was formed on 10 December 1944 with men from the

31st Infantry Division 'Calabria' and the 35th Artillery Regiment, with volunteers recruited later, to replace casualties. It supplied the 1st Special Service Force and the 34th Infantry Division on the Cassino front and later the 85th Division at Minturno. After a period of rest, it rejoined the 85th Division on the 'Gothic' Line. In January 1945, the 5th Pack Unit was attached to the 10th Mountain Division for which it worked until the end of the war. Later, Captain Galli, the unit's commander, received the following letter:

10th Mountain Division
Office of the Commanding General

APO 345, U. S. Army
17 June 1945

1.   It gives me great pleasure to be able to personally commend you, Captain Galli, your officers, and the men of your command for the continuous superior performance of duty from the time your command was attached to the 10th Mountain Division until the final collapse of the German Army saw our combined efforts crowned with victory.

2.   The performance of duty, the excellence of military courtesy and discipline and the *esprit de corps* of your command were at all times excellent. I recall now, some of the tasks that were performed by your command under the personal supervision of yourself and the officers of your command. In the initial attack on Campiano Ridge, it was necessary to move a 75 millimeter howitzer to the ridge to reduce enemy artillery that fired from Farne. Seven men of your command packed, dragged, and pushed that howitzer up the precipitous trail to where it was able, not only to neutralize the fire from Farne but also to put flanking fire on the enemy lines that were holding Mt. Belvedere. The key positions to the Mt. Belvedere sector was Mt. Della Torraccia. When Mt. Della Torraccia was taken, the men of your command moved ammunition and supplies to the front line positions in such quantity and with such speed that our troops were able to completely destroy a major German counter-attack. In the final attack, which was opened April 14, you were supporting the 85th Mountain Infantry in one of the most heavily mined and desperately defended sectors of our front. Words cannot describe the courage that was necessary to keep a continuous flow of supply moving to our attacking troops, yet your men were constantly and courageously moving ammunition and rations forward until the German resistance completely collapsed and we poured through his disorganized position into the Po Valley.

3.   The performance of your command is worthy of the fine tradition of all Allied Arms and an example of Service, Courage, and Leadership and on behalf of the 10th Mountain Division, I wish to thank you for a job well done.

*GEORGE P. HAYS*
Major General U. S. Army
Commanding

This is one of twenty-three similar letters received by the 5th Pack Unit Headquarters from American corps, divisions and regiments to which they were attached during the campaign. With one of the last letters, quoted below, came a parcel containing 5th Army shoulder patches.

Headquarters
2695th Technical Supervision Regt.

APO 464, U.S. Army
31 May 1945

1.   It gives me pleasure to issue to the 5th Italian Pack Mule Company, 5th Army shoulder patches to be worn by your officers and men.
2.   These patches are issued to your company because its discipline, spirit, sanitation and care of its equipment have met the standards of the 5th Army.

J. S. WINSLOW,
Lt.Col., FA,
Commanding.

The privilege of wearing an Allied Army badge was granted before to the Polish units that captured Montecassino.

## THE FINAL OFFENSIVE

The 15th Army Group lined up the following divisions, from west to east, for the final offensive:

Michael Goode, A/B AA3 Rating, Royal Navy, in a photograph taken in 1945, at the age of eighteen already a war veteran with three ribbons, the last of which is the Italy Star. *R. Goode Collection*

**15th Army Group**
US 5th Army
4th Corps
  92nd Infantry Division 'Buffalo'
  Task Force 45
  Brazilian Expeditionary Force
  10th Mountain Division
  1st Armored Division
  442nd and 473rd Infantry Regiments
2nd Corps
  6th South African Armoured Division
  88th Infantry Division 'Blue Devil'
  91st Infantry Division 'Powder River'
  34th Infantry Division 'Red Bull'
  Combat Group 'Legnano'

Reserve
  85th Infantry Division 'Custer'
  Combat Group 'Mantova'

British 8th Army
13th Corps
  10th Indian Division
  Combat Group 'Folgore'
10th Corps
  Jewish Brigade Group
  Combat Group 'Friuli'
2nd Polish Corps
  3rd Carpathian Rifle Division
  5th Kresowa Infantry Division
  2nd Armoured Brigade (Polish)
  7th Armoured Brigade
5th Corps
  2nd New Zealand Division
  8th Indian Division
  56th (London) Division
  78th Infantry Division
  Combat Group 'Cremona'
  2nd Armoured Brigade (British)
  9th Armoured Brigade
  21st Tank Brigade
  No 2 Commando

Reserve
  6th Armoured Division
  2nd Parachute Brigade

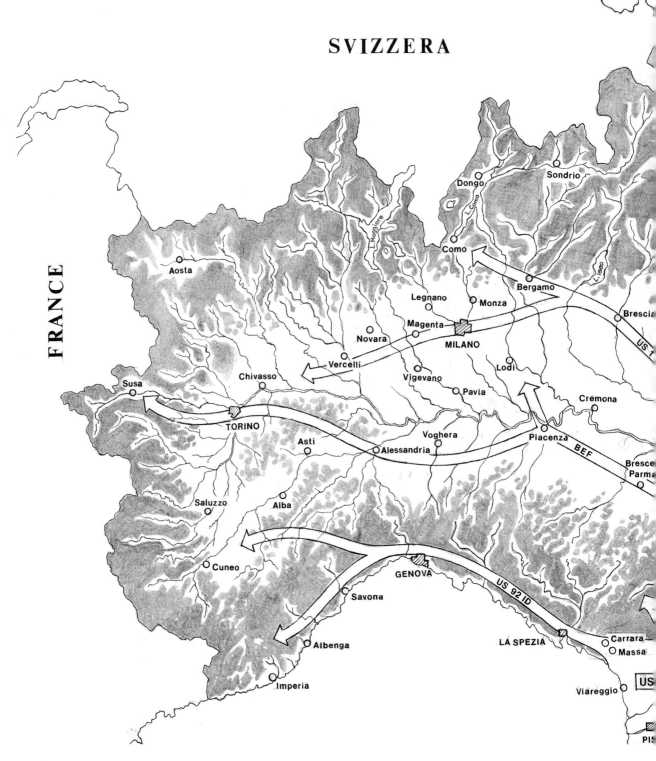

SVIZZERA

FRANCE

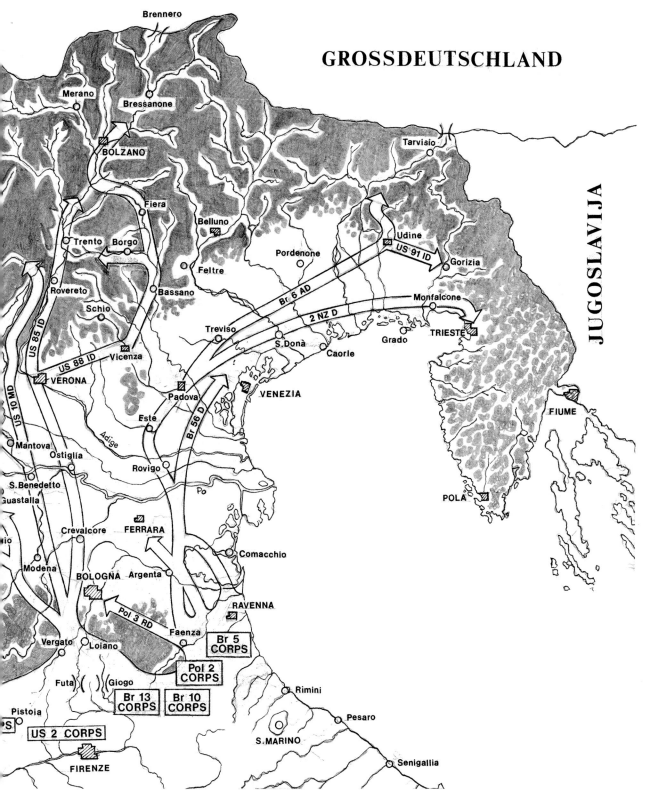

## 8th Army

The Allied offensive began with preliminary attacks against the Germans' right flank, towards the Ligurian coast, but the real offensive started on 9 April when a tremendous artillery bombardment crushed the first defensive line on the Senio. The Allied air force took care of the line on the Santerno river and others that the Germans had prepared during the winter.

The New Zealanders, the Indians and the Italians of the 'Cremona' crossed the Senio, captured Alfonsine on Highway 16 and two days later breeched the Santerno line of defences. On 15 April, the New Zealanders reached the Sillaro river and the 10th Indian Division was ordered to join them.

Meanwhile, the 167th Brigade of 56th Division was ferried across the Comacchio lake, by-passing the German defences on the Reno river to secure control of the Argenta Gap in which Highway 16 ran northwards.

Although fierce opposition was encountered as the Germans seemed determined to defend their positions to the end, the Allied advance continued. The 6th Armoured Division joined the New Zealanders leading towards Ferrara and the Po river. The 2nd Polish Corps and the Combat Group 'Friuli' moved towards Imola, which was captured on 14 April, and proceeded towards Bologna following the direction of Highway 9.

## 5th Army

The 5th Army offensive, scheduled to begin on 12 April, was delayed until the 14th by bad weather impeding air support. The operation gravitated towards the area between Modena and Bologna defended by 14th Panzer Corps on the left and 1st Parachute Corps on the right. At this stage, the latter comprised the 65th and the 305th Division only because all available forces had been drawn into the battle on the Adriatic sector.

The 4th Corps moved towards Montesi and Susano, with the 10th Mountain Division engaged in the task of dislodging the Germans from their higher positions, in a first phase of the operations aimed to reach the so-called 'Green' Line. The 2nd Corps advanced on its right flank on both sides of Highway 65.

The 'Brown' Line had to be reached next, about six miles north of Vergato, with the 6th South African Armoured Division towards Mount Sole and with the Americans going for Monterumici, Mount Adone and Pianoro. The 88th and 91st Divisions became involved in a sharp battle for these localities, and for the village of Livignano. Mount Adone was taken on 18 April. The same day, the 85th Division replaced the 1st Armored Division in the 4th Corps' area.

The German 334th Division of 51st Corps gave way on the American left flank and three divisions, the 1st Armored, 10th Mountain and 85th Infantry exploited the situation. The latter captured Caselecchio di Reno on 19 April and the 88th 'Blue Devil' captured Riale as both American corps drove into the Po valley aiming for Highway 9.

Staff Sergeant Gerald Tessier, 350th Infantry Regiment, 88th Infantry Division 'Blue Devil', later in the 351st 'TRUST'. After the war US Army senior NCOs, from the 3rd Grade upwards, started to wear OD dark shade, garrison caps. *G. Rosignoli Collection*

General von Vietinghoff asked, again, for permission to retreat to the Po river because time was running out and his Army Group 'C' was on the verge of being destroyed. Most German units were already retreating, having lost their defensive positions. The 5th and the 8th Army met at Finale Emilia, on the Panaro river, the 16th/5th Lancers from the east and units from the 11th South African Brigade from the west, trapping most of the German 76th Panzer Corps in between.

There were no more lines to stop the Allies' advance.

---

**Krauts and medics**

'The Krauts showed no mercy to medics and frequently took advantage of Geneva Convention rules to advance infantrymen under the protection of Red Cross insignia and armbands.

'"One time I was trying to reach a wounded man and a sniper kept firing at me" reported Pfc Alfred Tavares of New Bedford, Massachusetts. "Every time I moved, he'd fire, I couldn't get to the wounded man and couldn't shoot back since medics are unarmed. Finally a lieutenant crawled up behind me, located the sniper and shot him. As soon as he was hit, the German came out with his hands up and surrendered, begging for the same mercy he had refused to show our wounded. Some of the guys wanted to kill him anyway, but they let him live.

'"Yes, they shot at medics and they shot to kill" Tavares continued. "I had some friends killed and they were shot right in the head – right through the center of the Red Cross insignia painted on their helmets. On the other hand the Germans never missed a chance to take advantage of American respect for the medical code. There were countless incidents along this line.

'"One I recall especially was the time four Germans under a Red Cross flag approached a lead rifle company, carrying a litter on which was an apparently wounded man. Our troops held their fire. The Germans tenderly carried the litter nearer and nearer – suddenly they jumped into a ditch, whipped off the blankets and disclosed the wounded man to be a machine gun which cut down several of our men before return fire killed the Kraut quartette."'

From *The Blue Devils in Italy* by John P. Delaney.

---

# 7 The Aftermath of War

The end of the war in Italy was bizarre. A top general of the SS, Karl Wolff, one of the war's instigators and a staunch supporter of Hitler's policies, was the man who approached the Allies asking for terms and who finally surrendered unconditionally. The agreement was signed at Caserta on 29 April, to become effective on 2 May.

No one bothered to inform the 'Duce', or his staff, leaving the whole of the Italian forces to their own destiny. The Italians had surrendered to the Allies in September 1943 because they felt unable to carry on in the war and wanted to spare the country from further destructions. The opposite had happened: the entire country had been destroyed. In the end, they felt that they had just been used, by both sides.

Perhaps many German soldiers felt the futility of Salerno, Cassino, Anzio, the 'Gothic' Line; all the suffering they endured,

---

**Pot shots**

'I come from a family of farmers; we had a small plot only and therefore my brothers and I worked as farm hands for the big property owners.

'During a sunny day in the early spring of 1945 I was tilling the soil with my brothers, and others. It was a very large farm on flat ground in the valley. Each field was surrounded by shallow ditches which prevented it from water-logging and a few single trees were planted to mark intersections of paths.

'Two aircraft appeared on the horizon flying towards us just above the trees; they were Allies' planes as none of ours had been seen for months. We looked at them as they swooped above and resumed working.

'We soon realised with some alarm that the aircraft were turning around for another dive and ran for cover towards the trees, although with hindsight it would have been wiser to jump in a ditch. But we had no previous experience, we were not soldiers!

'My brother and I, safely under a tree, saw the aircraft approaching with their machine guns in action, the noise was terrifying, I looked at him, he was still standing nearby, one of his arms had been ripped off from the shoulder by a bullet.

'He did not hear any noise, the bullet hit him before he heard the noise of the machine guns.'

Tilio, Restaurant Owner, Capriva, near Gorizia.

---

Ninetyfirsters from the 316th Engineers at Naples on 10 September 1945 going home. *R. Livengood Collection*

the killing and destruction they inflicted upon others, all the waste. And they had still lost the war.

The fast manoeuvres of *Blitzkrieg* days were in the past. Most Germans units had horse-drawn carts; oxen often had to be used in lieu of horses. Tanks had to be left behind for lack of fuel.

The Allied advance was hampered mainly by the manner in which all roads were blocked by German convoys in retreat, but it was not a bloodless chase, as German units, true to their faith, set up defensive positions anywhere they could, even after the date of the cease-fire.

Bologna was the first major city to fall to the 3rd Carpathian Division on the morning of 21 April. The 10th Mountain Division reached the Po river, at San Benedetto, on Sunday, 22 April, and immediately crossed it in assault boats under fire from the opposite bank. On the following day, the US 85th, 88th and 91st Divisions and the South Africans reached the river and began crossing it.

The Brazilian Expeditionary Corps and the US 1st Armored and 34th Infantry became involved in a series of confrontations with German units trying to escape from the western Appennines. The 'Red Bulls' captured Parma during the night of 25 April, where a raiding party from the 1st Armored Division had caused havoc two days earlier. The whole of 1st Armored Division crossed the Po at San Benedetto and, through Brescia and Bergamo, the spearhead of the division reached Como during the morning of 28 April. The reconnaissance squadron proceeded westwards, by-passing Milan to the north, while Combat Command 'B' entered the city on 30 April. Vercelli and Novara were occupied by the 1st Armored Division which, on 2 May, began the task of disarming about thirty thousand Germans left in that north-western pocket.

The 92nd 'Buffalo' Division occupied the Ligurian coast. The Brazilian Expeditionary Force intercepted and surrounded the 148th German Division near Fornovo di Taro, south of Parma; it surrendered on 30 April, together with Italian troops. The Brazilians proceeded through Piacenza, Alessandria and Turin, arriving at Susa, near the French-Italian frontier, on 2 May.

The Allies' advance in north-eastern Italy had two objectives: to halt the retreating Germans before they could reach Austria to be reorganised on another defensive line; and to reach the furthest Italian region of Venezia Giulia before the Yugoslav Liberation Army.

During the night of 25 April, the 351st Infantry Regiment of the 88th Division arrived in the suburbs of Verona, and the 10th Mountain Division captured the airfield of Villafranca. The following day, the 85th Division began crossing the Adige river, followed by the 91st Division and the 6th South African Division. Further south, the British 6th Armoured Division and the New Zealanders formed the spearhead of the 8th Army's advance and, on 30 April, American and South African units met the 6th

Armoured Division at Treviso. The bulk of the German Army Group 'C' was trapped in the Po valley.

Subsequently, the 85th and 88th Divisions raced towards the Brenner pass and at 1051 hours on 4 May 1945, the Mediterranean and European Theatres of Operations joined up when the 349th Infantry Regiment, nicknamed the 'Krautkillers', made contact with patrols from the 103rd Division, 6th Corps, US 7th Army, a few miles south of the pass. Meanwhile, the British 6th Armoured Division blocked the Tarvisio pass and the 2nd New Zealand Division arrived in Trieste.

## THE CLNAI

The National Liberation Committee of Northern Italy ordered the general insurrection on 25 April in order to prevent the Germans from destroying everything in their path of retreat, as was their custom. They were known to have plans for scorched-earth measures which had to be prevented. Armed units of partisans occupied public buildings, factories, water works and power stations, chasing out the German rearguards and defusing their mines.

The Germans wanted to surrender to Allied units only and the partisans rarely managed to overpower their resistance. On the Allies' arrival, most cities were already under the CLNAI control and administration, the representatives of which were reluctant to be subordinate to the AMG and to the officials from the central government.

The CLNAI decided to settle its own scores with their former Italian rulers who were not to be handed over to the Allies or to the Carabinieri of the AMG but had to be put on trial by those whom they had persecuted. People's courts were set up in every

The 'Alexander's Diploma' No 124988, granted to Romano Triani (Blanco) in the name of the governments and people of the United Nations. *Patteri Collection*

town and village and the local fascists and captured personnel from the fascist armed forces were summarily brought to justice, and shot.

Mussolini, his mistress Claretta Petacci and several members of the Republican Fascist Government were captured on 27 April by the partisans of the 52nd Brigade at Dongo, on lake Como. All were executed and their bodies were brought to Milan and exposed to public view in Piazzale Loreto, where fifteen partisans had been executed in August 1944.

During the last days of the war, the Resistance movement was swollen by opportunists who picked up weapons discarded by Italian and German troops. In each area, a committee was formed by AMG officials, representatives of the CLN Military Branch and of the Italian War Ministry, with the task of questioning the partisans' leaders in order to select the real patriots who had fought during the war. A certificate for merit, known as the 'Alexander's Diploma', was granted to these men and women at a special military ceremony in commemoration of the end of the war. After the ceremony, the partisans handed in their weapons.

## THE VENEZIA GIULIA

At this stage, however, the most serious situation was developing in the eastern region of Venezia Giulia, most of which had been already occupied by the Yugoslav Liberation Army, contrary to international agreements.

In the west, the French Army had occupied parts of Italian territory, but as 15th Army Group only was supposed to control all Italy within its prewar frontiers, the French withdrew. The Yugoslavs set up their own military administration in their occupied territories, annexing them to Yugoslavia.

The British Government had guessed that problems would arise in the east, and forecast a dangerous situation when it was realised that Marshal Tito was pushing most of his army towards Italy. The 7th, 9th and 11th Partisan Corps were behind the German lines, and the 9th was already in Italian territory.

The powerful Yugoslav 'IX Korpus' absorbed the Italian communist partisan units in that area and replaced them with Yugoslav units. Only the 'Osoppo' Brigade, who were non-communist, had refused to merge. Therefore, its commander and staff were killed in an ambush in February 1945.

On 30 April, General Freyberg's 2nd New Zealand Division, still on the Piave river, was ordered to secure possession of the port of Trieste and the town of Gorizia which were to become part of the supply lines of the British forces in Austria. On the Isonzo river, the New Zealanders were met by Yugoslav and communist red flags, not by the usual spontaneous popular enthusiasm. In Trieste, they received the surrender of the German garrison, which had refused to surrender to the communists. Allied units entered Gorizia while the Yugoslavs, disregarding their presence, set up their own administration in the whole region.

The two armies were not on friendly terms. As the US 361st Infantry Regiment, for example, was moving to Tarnova, northeast of Gorizia, the commanding officer of the 13th Yugoslav Division ordered the Americans to withdraw or he would force them out.

The US 2nd Corps and the British 13th Corps were moved to the west bank of the Isonzo, ready to intervene. On 10 May, Field Marshal Alexander, Supreme Allied Commander Mediterranean, sent his chief of staff, Lt General W. D. Morgan, to Belgrade to discuss the situation with Marshal Tito.

Soon the controversy reached diplomatic levels in London and Washington. Finally, the Belgrade Agreement was signed on 9 June and the Yugoslav forces were ordered to yield part of Venezia Giulia to the AMG. General Morgan for the Allies and General Jovanovic for the Yugoslav High Command settled the demarcation line between their forces, which became known as the 'Morgan' Line.

On 12 June, the Yugoslav Liberation Army withdrew behind its new frontier and the AMG XIII Corps, later called AMG-Venezia Giulia took office.

## AMG IN ITALY

After the end of the war, on 5 May 1945, the provinces of northern Tuscany became part of Region VIII and five days later, the provinces of Siena, Grosseto and Arezzo and the regions of Umbria and Marche were returned to the Italian administrations. Tuscany and the region of Emilia were returned on 4 August. The ports of Naples and Leghorn remained under Allied administration until the end of December.

Throughout the invasion of Italy, the Allies had the dual responsibility of looking after their own armies and the population of the newly-occupied territories. The Italian Government could do very little as everything had either been destroyed by warfare or abducted by the withdrawing armies. Even when supplies could be obtained the Allies had to distribute them with their own transport.

The 5th Army AMG at the time of the occupation of Rome had under its command an Italian truck unit equipped with one hundred and forty vehicles and a British unit with thirty to supply the capital at the rate of some three hundred tons a day from the dump at Anzio. It had also to meet the increasing requirements of other areas as the Allied troops were rapidly advancing northwards.

The regions of Umbria, Marche and the south of Tuscany were relatively self-sufficient in food supplies. In contrast more urban areas south of the 'Gothic' Line, densely populated and full of refugees, had little resources as the Germans had destroyed anything they could not remove.

The final invasion of northern Italy had confronted the Allies with serious problems. The area was large, densely populated, badly damaged by warfare already and doomed to be in an even worse state after the final battles. The population was highly politicised. Moreover, after the 15th Army Group had defeated the Germans, the Allies would have been responsible for the survival of hundreds of thousands of prisoners of war. They included Germans, Italians, Russians and Yugoslavs – not to mention the Italian partisans, armies of them, who had to be disarmed.

To simplify the organisation of the vast administrative and logistical task looming ahead, the whole territory of Italy was divided into three military districts in March 1945. The 1st District comprised the north-east and the eastern side of central Italy, including the provinces of Terni, Perugia and Ascoli Piceno, under British responsibility. The 2nd District, under the Americans, comprised the north-western regions. In between these two districts was the area of the US Peninsular Base Section which formed a corridor from the port of Leghorn to the Brenner pass for the lines of communication of the US Forces in Austria. Sardinia was also part of 2nd District. The 3rd District comprised the southern regions and Sicily.

At the beginning of June 1945, the north-eastern regions, except Venezia Giulia and the troops stationed there, passed under the jurisdiction of 1st District, as the 8th Army moved to Austria. The 2nd District became operational in mid-July.

The provinces of Udine, Gorizia and Trieste, and the city of Pola, in the peninsula of Istria, remained under the military administration of the AMG of 13th Corps until 1947. Owing to the Peace Treaty, signed in Paris in February 1947, Gorizia and Udine were assigned to Italy, Pola to Yugoslavia, and the Free Territory of Trieste was created. It remained under Allied occupation, until 26 October 1954, when the city and most of 'A' Zone were restored to Italy.

The Italians and the Allies had a long relationship, usually friendly. The British 24th Infantry Brigade (Guards) and the US 351st Infantry Regiment had arrived in Italy at the end of 1943 and remained there for almost eleven years.

They did a good job!

---

**Return to the battlefield**

'Three years ago my wife and I spent a couple of weeks in Loiano. We had a wonderful time there but did not venture too far back into the mountains.

'What a stark contrast between the Italy of today and the Italy of forty-three years ago! The drive from Florence to Bologna is beautiful. Many places I couldn't remember at all. I found Pietramala least changed of all the old towns along Highway 65. The ancient palace is now deserted and empty and cold and forlorn looking; its rooms dark, dismal and gloomy. The town looks and feels old.

'We stopped on several occasions and had a glass of wine at a small "ristorante" and as I sat there I almost expected to see puptents in the fields or perhaps a company kitchen in one of the yards, or a platoon of infantry marching up the street.

'Outside the town, the old United States Cemetery had become a patch of bright yellow flowers. After the war, all the bodies of the Americans were taken to the Florence Cemetery.'

Roy Livengood, formerly in the 'Powder River' gang from Company 'E', 363rd Infantry Regiment, US 91st Infantry Division.

---

ALLIED FORCE HEADQUARTERS

*2 May, 1945*

## SPECIAL ORDER OF THE DAY

### Soldiers, Sailors and Airmen of the Allied Forces in the Mediterranean Theatre

After nearly two years of hard and continuous fighting which started in Sicily in the summer of 1943, you stand today as the victors of the Italian Campaign.

You have won a victory which has ended in the complete and utter rout of the German armed forces in the Mediterranean. By clearing Italy of the last Nazi aggressor, you have liberated a country of over 40,000,000 people.

Today the remnants of a once proud Army have laid down their arms to you—close on a million men with all their arms, equipment and impedimenta.

You may well be proud of this great and victorious campaign which will long live in history as one of the greatest and most successful ever waged.

No praise is high enough for you sailors, soldiers, airmen and workers of the United Forces in Italy for your magnificent triumph.

My gratitude to you and my admiration is unbounded and only equalled by the pride which is mine in being your Commander-in-Chief.

*H.R. Alexander*

*Field-Marshal,*
*Supreme Allied Commander,*
*Mediterranean Theatre.*

The Order of the Day issued by Field Marshal Alexander on 2 May 1945, which commemorates the end of the war in Italy.

# Bibliography

## HISTORICAL

ANDERS, GENERAL WLADISLAV *An Army in Exile* Macmillan, London 1949
ANONYMOUS *Teheran to Trieste* R. W. Pearce, Bombay, India

CARVER, BRIGADIER R. M. P. *The History of the 4th Armoured Brigade* Gale and Polden, Aldershot 1945
CLARK, GENERAL MARK WAINE *Calculated Risk* Harper, New York 1950
CROW, DUNCAN *British and Commonwealth Armoured Formations 1919–46* Profile Publications Ltd, Windsor 1971
CUNNINGHAM, ADMIRAL OF THE FLEET, VISCOUNT OF HYNDHOPE *A Sailor's Odyssey* E. P. Dutton & Co. Inc., New York, USA 1951

DELANEY, JOHN P. *The Blue Devils in Italy* 88th Infantry Division Association, New York

FAIRRIE, LIEUTENANT COLONEL ANGUS *Cuidich 'n Righ* Regimental HQ The Queen's Own Highlanders, Inverness, Scotland 1983
FARRAN, ROY *Winged Dagger* Fontana/Collins, London and Glasgow 1971

GRAHAM, DOMINICK *Cassino* Ballantine, New York, USA 1971
— AND BIDWELL, S. *Tug of War, The Battle for Italy: 1943–45* Hodder & Stoughton, London 1986
GREGORY, BARRY *British Airborne Troops* Macdonald and Jane's, London 1974
— AND BATCHELOR, JOHN *Airborne Warfare 1918–1945* Phoebus, London 1979

HAMMERTON, SIR JOHN AND GWYNN, MAJ. GENERAL SIR CHARLES *The Second World War* nine volumes, The Waverley Book Company Ltd – The Amalgamated Press, London

HARRIS, C. R. S. *Allied Military Administration of Italy* Her Majesty's Stationery Office, London 1957
HORSFALL, JOHN *Fling our Banner to the Wind* The Roundwood Press Ltd, Kineton 1978

JOSLEN, LIEUTENANT COLONEL H. F. *Orders of Battle* Her Majesty's Stationery Office, London 1961
LE MAREC, BERNARD *Les Francais Libres et Leurs Emblemes* Charles-Lavauzelle & Cie, Limoges, France 1964
LISIANI, VLADIMIRO *Good-bye Trieste* Mursia, Milano, Italy 1966
MOLLO, BORIS *The Sharpshooters* Historical Research Unit, London 1970
MONTGOMERY, FIELD MARSHAL, VISCOUNT OF ALAMEIN *Memoirs* Fontana, London 1960

NEVILLE, LIEUTENANT COLONEL SIR J. E. N., *editor The Oxfordshire and Buckinghamshire Light Infantry Chronicle* Gale & Polden, Aldershot 1951
NICHOLSON, G. W. L. *The Canadians in Italy, Official History of the Canadian Army in the Second World War* Queen's Printer, Ottawa, Canada 1956

OFFICIAL *Esercito Italiano* Stato Maggiore dell'Esercito, Ufficio Storico, Roma, Italy 1962
— *Combat Divisions of World War Two* Army Times, Washington DC, USA

PENIAKOFF, LIEUTENANT COLONEL VLADIMIR *Private Army* Jonathan Cape, London 1950
PISANO, GIORGIO *Gli ultimi in Grigio Verde* Edizioni F. P. E., Milano, Italy 1967
— *Para* Edizioni F.P.E., Milano, Italy 1968

RAY, CYRIL *Algiers to Austria* Eyre & Spottiswoode, London 1953

SAUNDERS, HILARY ST GEORGE  *The Red Beret* Michael Joseph Ltd, London 1950
— *The Green Beret*  New English Library, London 1971
SAWICKI, JAMES A.  *Infantry Regiments of the US Army*  Wyvern Publications, Dumfries, Scotland 1981
— *Field Artillery Battalions*  two volumes, Wyvern Publications, Dumfries, Scotland. Vol 1 1977, Vol 2 1978
STEVENS, LIEUTENANT COLONEL G. R. *Fourth Indian Division*  McLaren & Son, Toronto, Canada 1946

TERLECKI, OLGIERD  *Poles in the Italian Campaign*  Rada Ochrony Pomnikow Walki i Meczenstwa, Warsaw, Poland 1972

WANKOWICZ, MELCHIO  *Bitwa o Monte Cassino*  three volumes, 1947

## INSIGNIA

COLE, LIEUTENANT COLONEL HOWARD N. *Heraldry in War*  Gale & Polden, Aldershot 1946
— *Badges on Battledress*  Gale & Polden, Aldershot 1953

DAVIS, BRIAN LEIGH  *British Army Uniforms and Insignia of World War Two*  Arms and Armour Press, London 1983

EDWARDS, MAJOR T. J.  *Regimental Badges* Gale & Polden, Aldershot 1957

GAYLOR, JOHN  *Military Badges Collecting* Seeley, Service & Co., London 1971

KIPLING, ARTHUR L., AND KING, HUGH L. *Head-dress Badges of the British Army*  two volumes, Frederick Muller Ltd, London, Vol 1 1973, Vol 2 1979

MASSARO, LIEUTENANT COLONEL JOSEPH M. *Distinctive Insignia of the US Army Air Forces 1924–1947*  International Publishing Co., Austin, USA 1987

ROSIGNOLI, GUIDO  *Badges and Insignia of World War 2* 'Blandford Colour Series', four volumes, Blandford Press, London and Poole:
   *Army Badges and Insignia Book 1*  1972;
   *Army Badges and Insignia Book 2*  1975;
   *Air Force Badges and Insignia*  1976;
   *Naval and Marine Badges and Insignia* 1980
— *Uniformi e distintivi della Polizia Civile AMG-VG and AMG-FTT*  Albertelli, Parma, Italy 1986

WARING, MAJOR JOHN  *Identification Pamphlet No 1*

## PERIODICALS AND MAGAZINES

*After the Battle*  Battle of Britain Prints International, London
*Militaria Magazine*  Historie et Collections, Paris, France
*Military Illustrated – Past & Present* Military Illustrated Ltd, London
*Rivista Militare*  Stato Maggiore dell'Esercito, Roma, Italy
*Storia Illustrata*  Arnoldo Mondadori Editore, Italy
*Uniformes*  Argout-Editions, Paris, France
*World War Two*  partwork, Orbis Publishing Ltd, London
*World War Two Journal*  Ray Merriam, Bennington, Vermont, Virginia, USA

# Acknowledgements

I would like to express my sincerest gratitude to all the friends who have generously helped me in the compilation of this book.

My special thanks are due to: Mr Hugh L. King and Mr John Lucas, who helped me throughout this work; Mr Krzysztof Barbarski, who provided all the information on the 2nd Polish Corps; Mr Bernard Jamin, who provided all the information on the French Expeditionary Corps; and Mr Joe Harper, who provided all the information on the Canadians; and to Lt Colonel D. Clayton, Mr Richard M. Fillery, Mr Michael E. Gonzales, Mr Roy Livengood, Mr Howard M. Simpson, Mr Harold B. Stokes, and Mr Stephen Wragg, who kindly lent me their photographs and war souvenirs.

I am grateful to the following individuals for their assistance: Mr Piero Crociani; Mr C. W. Hill; Mr Colin Larmer; Mr Norman Lichfield. Lieutenant Colonel Joseph M. Massaro (Ret); Colonel Evan Murdock (Ret); Mr Mario Pace; Mr 'Wally' Pooley; Squadron Leader A. J. A. Roberts, DFC, RAF; Mr Terry J. Sampson; and Commandant H. Smit.

I am indebted to the following organisations for their assistance during research: Airborne Forces Museum; Lancashire County Council; Leicestershire Museums; London Irish Rifles Regimental Museum; National Museums and Galleries on Merseyside; New Zealand Ministry of Defence Army General Staff Defence Headquarters; The Polish Institute and Sikorski Museum; Princess Louise's Kensington Regimental Association; the Regimental Headquarters of The Argyll and Sutherland Highlanders, The Gordon Highlanders, The Green Howards, and The Royal Irish Rangers; Regimental Museum XV/XIX The King's Royal Hussars; The Royal Air Force Museum; The Royal Artillery Institution; The Royal British Legion; The Royal Engineers Museum; The Royal Hampshire Museum; The Royal National Army Museum; Scottish United Services Museum; South African National Museum of Military History; the Embassy of the United States of America in London; the US 1st Armored Division Association; the US 45th Infantry Division Museum; the US 91st Infantry Division Association; and The Warwickshire Yeomanry Museum.

Many thanks to my wife Diana for her invaluable help.

G. ROSIGNOLI

# Index